W9-ALJ-257

DISCARD

DISCARD

Economics

Volume 3

The citizen and the economy

GROLIER
EDUCATIONAL

Sherman Turnpike,
Danbury, Connecticut
06816

Published 2000 by Grolier Educational
Sherman Turnpike
Danbury, Connecticut 06816

© 2000 Brown Partworks Ltd

Set ISBN: 0-7172-9492-7
Volume ISBN: 0-7172-9484-6

For information address the publisher:
Grolier Educational, Sherman Turnpike,
Danbury, Connecticut 06816

FOR BROWN PARTWORKS LTD

Project editor:
Jane Lanigan
Editors: Tim Cooke, Julian
Flanders, Mike Janson,
Henry Russell
Editorial assistance:
Wendy Horobin,
Tim Mahoney,
Sally McEachern,
Chris Wiegand
Design: Tony Cohen,
Bradley Davis,
Matthew Greenfield
Picture research:
Helen Simm
Graphics: Mark Walker
Indexer: Kay Ollerenshaw

Project consultant: Robert
Pennington, Associate
Professor, College of
Business Administration,
University of Central Florida
Text: Amanda Friedenberg,
Justine Burns, Malcolm
Keswell, Richard Johnson,
Bruce Rayton

About this book

Economics is all around us. It covers almost
every aspect of life today, from how much
money you have in your pocket to the price of
real estate, from how much tax people pay to
the causes of wars in distant lands. In today's
world it is essential to understand how to manage your money, how to save wisely, and how
to shop around for good deals. It is also important to know the bigger picture: how financial
institutions work, how wealth is created and
distributed, how economics relates to politics,
and how the global economy works that ties
together everyone on the planet.

Economics places everyday financial
matters in the wider context of the sometimes
mysterious economic forces that shape our
lives, tracing the emergence of economic doc-
trines and explaining how economic systems
worked in the past and how they work now.

Each of the six books covers a particular area of economics, from personal finance to
the world economy. Five books are split into
chapters that explore their themes in depth.
Volume 5, Economic Theory, is arranged as an A-
Z encyclopedia of shorter articles about fundamental concepts in economics and can be used
as an accessible reference when reading the
rest of the set. At the end of every chapter or
article a See Also box refers you to related articles elsewhere in the set, allowing you to further investigate topics of particular interest.

The books contain many charts and
diagrams to explain important data clearly and
explain their significance. There are also special
boxes throughout the set that highlight particular subjects in greater detail. They might explain
how to fill out a check correctly, analyze the
theory proposed by a particular economist, or
tell a story that shows how economic theory
relates to events in our everyday lives.

If you are not sure where to find a
subject, look it up in the set index in each
volume. The index covers all six books, so it
will help you trace topics throughout the set.
There is also a glossary at the end of the book,
which provides a brief explanation of some of
the key words and phrases that occur throughout the volumes. The extensive Further Reading
list contains many of the most recent books
about different areas of economics to allow you
to do your own research. It also features a list
of useful web sites where you can find up-to-
date information and statistics.

Contents

The citizen and the economy

Government and the economy

It is generally agreed in modern society that governments have to balance the following macroeconomic aims: full employment, stable price levels, a high level of growth in the economy, and keeping imports and exports in balance. Their role is in choosing how to achieve these goals.

Governments exist in all national economies, so it is natural to expect the government to act as an economic policy-maker. Rarely does the public question that the government has a role to play. However, the public is likely to question the government's priorities and its choice of policy.

What do governments do?

Governments are generally said to have four major macroeconomic goals:
● to maintain full employment;
● to keep price levels stable;
● to achieve a high level of growth in the economy;
● to keep imports and exports in balance.

In terms of microeconomics there is also a role for government in the provision of public goods and merit or mixed goods, while some argue that governments also have a responsibility to ensure some kind of equitable distribution of income in the economy (*see* Government and the individual, page 28). Further microeconomic goals include maintaining competition in markets and regulating the environmental impacts of economic activity (*see* Government and business, page 43).

A government must choose the direction of its broad economic policy. This choice ranges from the free market, which imposes minimum government intervention, to a command economy, where the state makes most resource-allocation decisions. In a democracy this policy choice is usually influenced by the need to achieve popularity for the next election. Since the economy affects the level of employment, inflation rates, the balance of payments, and growth rates, all seen as crucial indicators of the health of a nation, a successful economic policy is likely to ensure reelection.

There are also different policy instruments a government might choose to achieve its economic goals. Fiscal policy, for example, involves changes in taxation and government spending to affect the overall level of demand

in the economy, while monetary policy involves manipulating the money supply, credit, and interest rates to achieve policy goals.

This chapter explores both the role of government as an economic policy-maker and its choice of policy. It then looks at the instruments the government might use to implement its particular objective.

ABOVE: The Capitol Building in Washington D.C., from where the U.S. government runs the most powerful economy in the world.

The Macroeconomy

Macroeconomics is the study of the general economics of a large unit such as a country. The relationship between individuals and firms is of chief importance in studying macroeconomics. Consumers are integral in providing revenue for firms via purchases; in turn, firms are important in providing income, in terms of wages, to the household. This codependence, illustrated in Figure 1, is called the circular income model. For the sake of simplicity this first model excludes investment by firms (i.e., borrowing to purchase new machinery and equipment), taxation, imports, and exports.

Investments are made possible through household savings. As individuals choose between consumption and savings, the financial system—banks, etc.—is given a role, which is to distribute savings to businesses for investment projects. In turn, investment in capital equipment enables firms to produce a larger level of national income; with the larger level of national income consumers have a larger sum that they can consume or save.

Similarly, taxation alters the simple circular flow since it adds the government sector to the equation. This influence subtracts from consumers' income by reducing individuals' take-home income. At the same time, with a source of revenue the government is able to offer transfer payments, such as welfare benefits, which add to consumer income. Further, via government spending on goods and services there is a higher demand for firms' products; this serves to increase demand and thereby increase national income.

In the circular income model national income is considered in a closed economy. When the economy is open, however, goods and services may enter and leave the country. As imports—goods entering the country—increase, part of consumption no longer goes to the country's firms but to firms in other countries. In contrast, when products are exported, and goods leave the country, the country's firms experience an increase in demand, selling to consumers abroad.

The second model, Figure 2, which includes investment, taxation, imports, and exports, is more complex than the first since it tries to mimic the real world more closely. It is still a fairly simple model of demand, however, and excludes some key factors. For example, taxation might only be on household income, but it might also be levied on investment and imports. Further, as it is, the model says nothing about which goods are purchased and which goods are not. By failing to differentiate in this way, it implicitly assumes there are no externalities; in other words, it assumes that consumption of a good does not impose positive or negative effects on others. If these effects should exist, goods may be under- or overprovided.

As a result, the circular flow model, as illustrated in both Figures 1 and 2, is limited to answering macroeconomic questions. It cannot be used, for example, to see how increases in taxation might alter national income as a whole.

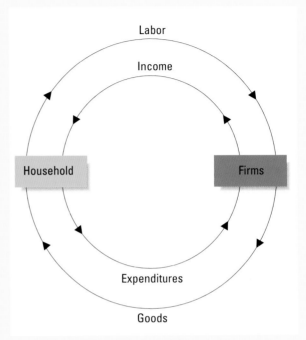

Figure 1 *The circular income model.*

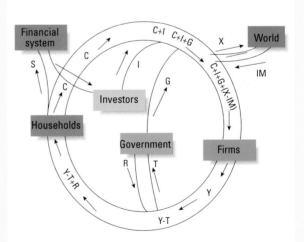

Figure 2 *The circular income model, including banking and the government sector.*

C = Consumer spending
G = Government expenditure
I = Investment
IM = Imports
R = Transfer payments
S = Saving
T = Taxes
Y = Income
X = Exports

The government as a policymaker

There are two standard reasons given for the necessary role of government in the economy: where market failure exists, and to redistribute income and wealth.

The redistribution of income and wealth is usually seen as desirable in a country where there are both rich and poor people. In this situation a natural system of justice seems to demand that the government should take from the rich and give to the poor. Market failure, on the other hand, is when the economy fails to achieve allocative efficiency—that is, it fails to supply the structure necessary for the most efficient satisfaction of peoples' wants and needs. Market failure may occur for a number of reasons, including anti-competitive practices by large firms, because of the existence of public goods, or as a result of externalities such as pollution .

Government is big business. In 1998 the U.S. government spent almost $1.4 trillion and employed more than 5 million people. During the last 60 years government spending in the United States has increased from 20 percent of the economy's total expenditure to 35 per cent. The government's role, then, has clearly become more important (*see* box page 20). However, perception of the success of any economic system is subjective, and people are often led to question the role of government in economic activity.

ABOVE: *A Rolls Royce parked outside a store on Rodeo Drive, Beverly Hills—a sight that may provoke dissatisfaction with the distribution of wealth in U.S. society.*

Healthcare reform in America

In 1993 President Clinton proposed healthcare reform in the form of universal healthcare coverage. The program, proposed as a result of the growing number of middle-income individuals who lacked insurance, would provide coverage via a health management organization (HMO). At the time, most of those covered by insurance did not participate in an HMO; they feared that with the passage of the bill they would require permission before visiting a doctor. Further, insurance companies did not like the proposal since it would provide competition. The initial state can be viewed as economically in equilibrium—no one could be made better off without others being made worse off. Because of opposition from those who would be made worse off, the reforms did not pass Congress.

Redistribution of wealth

One explanation for people's dissatisfaction is that society may not like the distribution implied by the price-quantity equilibrium. For example, the equilibrium might be such that one person gets 90 percent of all goods and services, while the remainder of society divides the balance of all other goods among them. Here, although the situation may be economically efficient, where no one can be made better off without the one rich individual losing goods, society may nonetheless be displeased by the outcome. Government may be required to improve on the distribution of wealth within the economy. Such programs might include welfare, Social Security, and food stamps.

Public goods

A second reason for government intervention is often cited as the need to provide public goods—goods or services each unit of which is consumed by everyone and from which no one can be excluded. Examples include the national defense system, the police, and fire services. Everyone in society benefits from national defense, no one can be excluded from these benefits, and one person's use of the service does not reduce its benefit for others. As a result of these characteristics, public goods have no market and no price; hence there is no motivation for private firms to provide them.

There is also an argument for government intervention in the provision of mixed or merit

goods, which lie between public and private goods. An example of a mixed good would be a highway, which is a public good until it becomes congested, at which point it becomes exclusive and therefore a mixed good. Other examples include education and health, which tend to be underprovided by the market mechanism.

Market failure and externalities

There is also a role for government where economic activities generate externalities and produce effects on the welfare of others. For example, an incinerator emits pollution, thereby resulting in a negative externality to those living or working nearby. Similarly, a park provides pleasure to those who view it, thus generating a positive externality; moreover, if no individual can be excluded from using the park, it is a public good.

When faced with an economy in which individuals value public, merit, or mixed goods, and goods exhibiting externalities, these goods will either be underprovided or overprovided. This results in market failure and the inefficient allocation of resources, where some individuals can be made better off without others being made worse off. In these cases government intervention will probably be necessary.

Although many economists accept this role of government, it is not entirely uncontroversial. An early critic, economist Ronald H. Coase, argued that market intervention by the government is not required if property rights have been assigned since the market will move to equilibrium by itself.

Suppose, for example, a firm pollutes a river that a farmer's cattle drinks from. Further, assume the firm has the property rights to do so. If the farmer's marginal cost is greater than the polluter's, the farmer will find it beneficial to pay off the firm so that it reduces its level of pollution. In doing so, an efficient outcome

ABOVE: *One method by which a government can redistribute wealth in society is by running a series of welfare programs, such as this food bank in Concord, California.*

LEFT: *These joggers are on their way to the local park in Los Angeles to take advantage of a local public good—the park. It is a public good because no one is excluded from it.*

will result where no one party can be made better off without another being worse off. This example illustrates the Coase Theorem that with well-defined property rights and a two-individual economy, the most efficient outcome will always result. Others have informally generalized this theorem by dropping the words "two-individual," thereby assuming that the result can occur in any economy with well-defined property rights.

More recently, it has been shown that the example is quite limited. When, for example, there is one polluter and a large number of farmers suffering the expense, the end need not be efficient because the farmers suffer a collective action problem. In this case they each have an incentive to shirk payment because they assume that other farmers have an incentive to pay.

Despite this argument and others, it is generally agreed among economists that the public accepts that there is a role for government in economic policymaking. It is therefore reasonable to ask what policies the government should adopt, the priority it should give those policies, and how it should pursue them. One popular answer is utilitarianism, which says that the government should seek the "greatest good for the greatest number." A second objective, the Rawlesian Social Welfare Function, seeks to maximize the value of the worst off individual.

Politics

Endemic to government, however, is politics. Politics can be seen as a system of individuals with varying degrees of policy-setting power, each trying to maximize their utility. Therefore, when analyzing the role of government as an economic policymaker, it is necessary to consider how government officials seek to set policy.

The goals of politicians are quite diverse; there is no consensus on how they choose to act. There are, however, three popular opinions. First, politicians are office-seeking—the intrinsic value of holding office leads politicians to desire obtaining a winning majority. Second, politicians are policy-oriented—their desire to be in office results from a genuine desire to achieve their preferred policy bundle. Third, politicians are rent-seeking—there are perks from office, such as providing contracting jobs to family members or accepting personal bribes, which cause politicians to seek office.

Political behavior differs according to the goals of the politician, as well as whether the politician can commit to implementing a particular policy after the election. It is also influenced by the timing of a governmental election, when the temptation to exploit the short-term trade-off between inflation and the unemployment rate for political advantage is often strong for some politicians.

ABOVE: U.S. Senator Phil Gramm, a Republican, speaks at a hearing of the Senate Budget Committee. This committee debates U.S. government spending, reaching consensus by a variety of political means.

Business cycles

A business cycle is an irregular periodic up-and-down movement in economic activity measured in the fluctuations of a country's GDP. This in itself is important to the government since it is an indicator of the current state of the country's economy. However, these cycles are also important for other reasons. Levels of unemployment, stock-market prices, and inflation are also closely tied to the business cycle. Technically, a business cycle is characterized by a peak, a trough, and a trend, and is not governed by the calendar. The peak is the highest level that output will reach in the given business cycle; in contrast, the trough is the lowest point of the cycle. A recession is a downturn in the level of economic activity; and if the trough is deep enough, it becomes a depression. Therefore business cycles, though random and unpredictable, are seen as crucial indicators of both the current state of the economy and of its future prospects.

Looking back at the history of the United States between 1876 and 1986, the growth rates of the economy have varied greatly between periods, as Figures 3a-c indicate. From 1919 through 1944 these changes were the most staggering. This period first suffered negative growth rates. In the roaring twenties this quickly changed as the economy saw its growth rates increase, at times in excess of 10 percent; however, this was to stop during the Great Depression. With the coming of World War II growth rates once again soared.

This volatile behavior comprises a business cycle. Table 1 on page 12 provides data on the number and length of cycles from 1854 to 1990. During this period there were 30 cycles. Since World War II there have been far fewer cycles than previously. Further, given the length of the period, there were relatively more cycles between World War I and World War II.

Peaks and troughs move about a trend. The trend in economic activity can change over time; this change usually occurs in the same direction and in a continuous manner. Figure 4 on page 13 illustrates a hypothetical pattern of a business cycle. As is evident, between the peak and the trough there is a period of decline, a recession. Similarly, between the trough and the subsequent peak output increases; this is a period of recovery.

Economists vary in opinion over the source of business cycles. The remainder of this section considers possible sources, ranging from animal spirits to technical shocks.

(i) The Keynesian business cycle

The economist John Maynard Keynes witnessed the Great Depression and sought to explain it. In doing so, he offered a theory of the business cycle that rests on investment behavior. In one of the most well-known books on economics, *The General Theory of Employment, Interest and Money* (1936), he wrote:

"Most, probably, of our decisions to do something positive, the full consequences of which will be drawn out over many

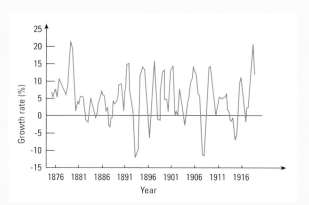

Figure 3a Growth rates in the U.S. economy, 1876-1918.

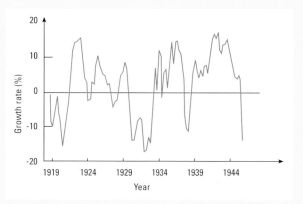

Figure 3b Growth rates in the U.S. economy, 1919-1945.

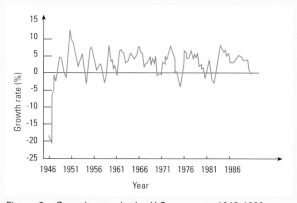

Figure 3c Growth rates in the U.S. economy, 1946-1986.

days to come, can only be taken as a result of animal spirits—of a spontaneous urge to action rather than inaction, and not as an outcome of a weighted average of quantitative benefits multiplied by quantitative probabilities. Enterprise only pretends to itself to be mainly actuated by the statements in its own prospectus, however candid and sincere. Only a little more than an expedition to the South Pole, is it based on an exact calculation of benefits to come. Thus, if the animal spirits are

| Business cycle reference dates | | Duration (months)* | | | |
| | | Contraction (trough from previous peak) | Expansion (trough to peak) | Cycle | |
Trough	Peak			Trough from previous trough	Peak from previous peak
December 1854	June 1857		30		
December 1858	October 1860	18	22	48	40
June 1861	April 1865	8	46	30	54
December 1867	June 1869	32	18	78	50
December 1870	October 1873	18	34	36	52
March 1879	March 1882	65	36	99	101
May 1885	March 1887	38	22	74	60
April 1888	July 1890	13	27	35	40
May 1891	January 1893	10	20	37	30
June 1894	December 1895	17	18	37	35
June 1897	June 1899	18	24	36	42
December 1900	September 1902	18	21	42	39
August 1904	May 1907	23	33	44	56
June 1908	January 1910	13	19	46	32
January 1912	January 1913	24	12	43	36
December 1914	August 1918	23	44	35	67
March 1919	January 1920	7	10	51	17
July 1921	May 1923	18	22	28	40
July 1924	October 1926	14	27	36	41
November 1927	August 1929	13	21	40	34
March 1933	May 1937	43	50	64	93
June 1938	February 1945	13	80	63	93
October 1945	November 1948	8	37	88	45
October 1949	July 1953	11	45	48	56
May 1954	August 1957	10	39	55	49
April 1958	April 1960	8	24	47	32
February 1961	December 1969	10	106	34	116
November 1970	November 1973	11	36	117	47
March 1975	January 1980	16	58	52	74
July 1980	July 1981	6	12	64	18
November 1982	July 1990	.16	.92	28	...
Average, all cycles:					
1854-1982 (30 cycles)		18	33	51	51
1854-1919 (16 cycles)		22	27	48	49
1919-1945 (6 cycles)		18	35	53	53
1945-1982 (8 cycles)		11	45	56	55
Average, peacetime cycles:					
1854-1982 (25 cycles)		19	27	46	46
1854-1919 (14 cycles)		22	24	46	47
1919-1945 (5 cycles)		20	26	46	45
1945-1982 (6 cycles)		11	34	46	44

*Underscored figures are the wartime expansions (Civil War, World Wars I and II, Korean War, and Vietnam War), the postwar contractions, and the full cycles that include wartime expansions.
Source: National Bureau of Economic Research, Inc.

Table 1 Business-cycle expansions and contractions in the United States, 1854-1990.

dimmed and the spontaneous optimism falters, leaving us to depend on nothing but a mathematical expectation, enterprise will fade and die; though fears of loss may have a basis no more reasonable than hopes of profit have before."

In other words, businesses form views about the future when they invest in capital equipment. When they calculate how much they are likely to get back in return for their investment, businesses have to make assumptions about future costs and future revenues. If business managers are feeling optimistic about the future, they will expect the return on their investment to be good, so planned investment will rise. If, on the other hand, they are more pessimistic, managers will expect the rate of return on investment projects to fall, and planned investment will go down.

Since investment is subject to these expectations—or "animal spirits"—the economy expects to see many shocks. A positive increase in investment spending by firms on equipment and machinery serves to increase output; this, in turn, increases the interest rate as demand for money to buy products increases. This increase in output is also associated with an increase in labor input; it reduces both the unemployment rate and labor productivity. Finally, the increase in investment shifts out the aggregate demand curve—representing the general level of demand in the economy—thereby increasing inflation.

Pure Keynesian analysis depends on animal spirits shifting in a patterned way in that a peak—when optimism is running high—tends to be followed by a trough, when business expectations are low.

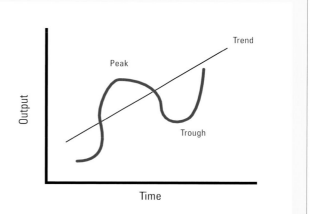

Figure 4 The hypothetical pattern of a business cycle.

(ii) Real business cycle theory

Real business cycle (RBC) theory assumes that the main sources of shocks to the economy are technological. So, for example, a shock in computer technology might mean that suddenly goods can be produced more effectively; aggregate supply—the general level of supply in the economy—is therefore greater. The shocks in these models must be temporary, but with a permanent aspect. When this is the case, individuals will substitute labor between periods; by working more in a boom, they can earn relatively more money than during a trough and, in the process, save for the future. Therefore, short-term output will increase.

Some have criticized this theory because it is difficult to

ABOVE: The Great Depression of the 1930s brought about unprecedented poverty and suffering to millions of people. It represented the most significant trough in American economic history. It is safe to say that J.M. Keynes' "animal spirits" were missing from economic policymakers minds during those years.

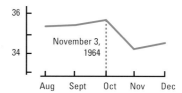

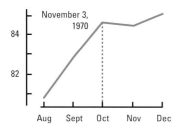

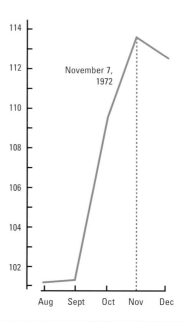

conceive of detrimental technology shocks. But one simple example of such a shock would be bad weather conditions— a tornado can ruin the productivity of crops in a given season. Advocates of RBC theory also point out that the level of technology need not decline for there to be detrimental effects on the economy. If only the growth in technological innovations declines, so that the economy does not gain greater improvements in computer technology, the economy can experience the same detrimental effects.

(iii) The Political business cycle

The explanations above indicate that government policy can increase economic activity in both the Keynesian and RBC framework. Under the Keynesian model government spending during a recession, for example, can increase aggregate demand in the economy and improve business expectations. Under the RBC model government expenditure will prompt an increase in labor supply and hence increases in output.

Political business cycle (PBC) models ask under what conditions the government will choose to instigate economic activity for political reasons. Models assume that individuals vote based on economic performance. Voting can be retrospective, where individuals vote based on how the economy performed during the incumbent's tenure in office, or prospective, where individuals vote based on how they envision future performance. In either case both office-seeking and policy-seeking politicians will be induced to stimulate economic activity so as to better obtain their objective.

There is a large amount of anecdotal evidence of the PBC. For example, Princeton University economist Edward R. Tufte, one of the early advocates of PBCs, quotes United States President Nixon as saying: "I knew from bitter experience how, in both 1954 and 1958, slumps which hit bottom early in October contributed to substantial Republican losses in the House and Senate. The power of the 'pocket-book' issue was shown more

Figure 5 Government transfer payments in relation to the date of the elections of 1962, 1964, 1970, and 1972 (billions of dollars, at seasonally adjusted annual rates).

Higher social security payments

Your social security payment has been increased by 20 percent, starting with this month's check, by a new statute enacted by the Congress and signed into law by President Richard Nixon on July 1, 1972.

The President also signed into law a provision which will allow your social security benefits to increase automatically if the cost of living goes up. Automatic benefit increases will be added to your check in future years according to the conditions set out in that law.

U.S. Department of Health, Education and Welfare
Social Security Administration
DHEW Publications No. (SSA) 73-10322
October 1972.

ABOVE: A letter sent out to Social Security beneficiaries before the U.S. presidential election in 1972 that indicates the government's desire to stimulate economic activity for political ends.

ABOVE: *Real business cycle theory assumes that the main source of shocks to the economy are technological. But the simplest shock could be provided by the weather. For example, severe conditions, such as a drought, can ruin the productivity of crops in any given season.*

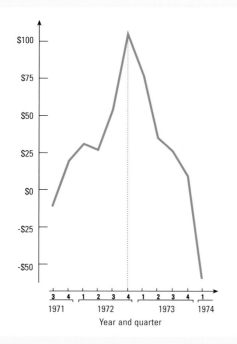

Figure 6 Quarterly changes in real disposable income surrounding the 1972 election.

clearly perhaps in 1958 than in any off-year election in history. On the international front, the Administration had one of its best years... Yet, the economic dip in October was obviously uppermost in people's minds when they went to the polls. They completely rejected the President's appeal for the election of

	Biennial periods	
	Before the presidential election	After the presidential election
For 1948-1976		
Rate of growth of money supply increased	4	1
Rate of growth of money supply decreased	3	6
For 1948-1976, except Eisenhower years		
Rate of growth of money supply increased	4	1
Rate of growth of money supply decreased	1	4

Table 2 The use of monetary policy before and after elections.

Republicans to the House and Senate" (Tufte, 1978).

This indicates that politicians do indeed consider economic stimulation to be necessary and important for winning the campaign. There is some evidence to suggest the politicians use policy instruments and output changes before the election. As seen in Figures 5 and 6 and Table 2, both fiscal and monetary policy have been used to stimulate the economy. Further, economic growth is often noticed prior to an election and a decline afterward, as demonstrated in Figure 6.

The government and macroeconomic policy

It has been suggested that the government sets its economic policies to maximize the welfare of society and to maximize the welfare of the politicians. This assumption makes the role of government as an economic policymaker by no means uncontroversial. Many, particularly in politics and the media, have declared a single goal to be desirable. This section attempts to explore some of the intuitive appeal and difficulties associated with particular policy goals.

Low unemployment

From a social policy standpoint low unemployment appears desirable and is regarded by the public as a crucial indicator of a successful and just society. Low, however, is an ambiguous term; it must be defined relative to some level. One thought is that unemployment should be defined relative to the natural rate—the long-run rate of unemployment to which the economy converges. If this is the case, then reducing the unemployment rate seems both desirable and feasible. Many who advocate a policy of low unemployment seek to implement a level of unemployment below the natural rate, however. Although on face value this seems like a desirable policy, upon closer inspection both the feasibility and the desirability of the policy are not clear.

In order to arrive at an understanding of this complicated concept, consider the Phillips Curve (see Figure 7). The Phillips Curve,

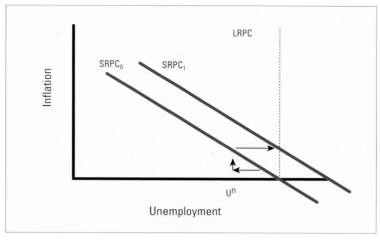

Figure 7 *When a low unemployment rate is implemented (U^n), expectations about real wages declining cause the short-run Phillips curve ($SRPC_0$) to shift outward ($SRPC_1$). Although the SRPC exhibits a trade-off between inflation and unemployment, in the long run the Phillips curve is vertical (LRPC).*

LEFT: *Shoppers also have to pay psychological costs in times of inflation. If shops adjust price labels up, then people feel worse off even if their incomes are keeping pace with the inflation rate.*

discovered in the midtwentieth century by New Zealand economist A.W. Phillips, was first presented as an observed phenomenon. Phillips noticed a trade-off between inflation (an upward movement in the price level) and unemployment in British data—as inflation went up, unemployment went down, and vice versa. This discovery was later confirmed in U.S. data, though it became suspect during the oil crisis of the 1970s, which saw both high inflation and high rates of unemployment. More importantly, the trade-off can be understood in light of the Keynesian aggregate supply and aggregate demand analysis. When aggregate demand shifts out due to an outside shock, both inflation and output rise. Because an increase in output requires an increase in labor input, unemployment must decrease. Therefore, Keynesian analysis explains the trade-off between inflation and unemployment.

However, it is argued that if the government attempts to implement an unemployment rate below the natural rate, it will merely result in a higher level of inflation but with no effect on employment.

Reduce inflation

Popular opinion, both among economists and individuals, is that inflation is bad and should, therefore, be reduced. As large as this consensus is, there is an equally large consensus among economists that there is no compelling explanation for the negative effects of inflation. One popular explanation is that individuals desire to know how much their costs will be at the time of retirement. If price levels are rising rapidly, it is difficult for people to judge their financial position in the future. In addition, if interest rates do not keep pace with inflation, people's savings will lose value. So inflation can be a disincentive to save.

Other explanations include psychological costs in that people feel they are worse off even if incomes are keeping pace with inflation. There are also "menu costs"—the fact that if there is inflation, restaurants have to change their menus to show increasing prices. Similarly, stores have to change price labels, vending machines have to be adjusted, and so on.

Another explanation rests on the assumption that with each trip to the bank, individuals incur costs—costs in terms of time, inconvenience, and so on. This being the case, with high levels of inflation individuals must visit the bank more often and incur greater costs. In addition, when there is a high rate of inflation, consumers and businesses are less sure what is a reasonable price level to pay, so have to do more "shopping around"—another cost. This explanation seems quite pleasing, especially in light of tales of hyperinflation—periods of extreme levels of inflation when people barely have time to collect their wages or take money from the bank before prices go up. However, it does not seem to indicate the detrimental effects imposed by low levels of inflation.

High growth rates

Intuitively, it seems that any country would prefer a higher level of output and therefore income. Since at least some individuals would be better off without others being made worse off, it appears that a higher level of output is an improvement. Therefore, it seems desirable for an economy to achieve a high growth rate and for the government to have this as a policy goal.

Economic growth is defined as the change in potential output of an economy; it is usually measured by the change in real national income. Economic growth generally results from improvements in the quantity and

Debate: democracy and growth

There have been many studies, both empirically and theoretically, exploring the relationship between economic liberties and growth. Recently, it has been shown that democracies do not increase long-term growth. However, they are associated with lower volatility of income and produce a more favorable income distribution (Rodrik, 1997). Theoretically, it is not clear why this is so. Some argue that democracies cause the more favorable economic outcomes, while others believe that favorable economic conditions lead to democracies (see Przeworski and Limongi, 1993).

quality of the factors of production—that is, improvements in the quantity and quality of land, labor, capital—and from technological progress. The government may seek to promote growth through, for example, putting money into the education and training of the workforce. Firms and businesses could be given favorable tax breaks, or the government might set a low interest rate to promote capital investment. The government might also invest in research and development into new production techniques or provide grants for firms and businesses to do so.

There is some debate, however, about the desirability of high economic growth rates—some economists argue that growth is the only possible cure to many of the world's serious economic ills, but others are convinced that growth causes the problems in the first place. A high growth rate can indicate that a country is rising toward a peak of a business cycle, which would therefore precede a period of decline. Or it might indicate

LEFT: One positive effect of a period of economic growth is government investment in the education and training of the workforce.

Reporting the National Income

In America the U.S. Department of Commerce compiles data on the country's income in the National Income and Product Account (NIPA), which is illustrated in Table 3 (right). NIPA offers information on numerous macroeconomic indicators, including GNP and GDP. GDP is a measure of the total flow of goods and services produced by a particular economy over a specified period of time, usually a year. It is measured by valuing total output at market prices. Only goods used for final consumption or investment (capital) goods are included. Income arising from investments and possessions owned by U.S. citizens abroad is not included in GDP, although income earned by foreigners in the domestic market is. GNP, on the other hand, is GDP plus income accruing to U.S. residents arising from investment abroad, minus income earned in the U.S. accruing to foreigners abroad.

There are two ways of reporting the gross product: in nominal terms and in real terms. The nominal product offers information on the number of goods and services by reporting the sum of goods times their specific prices. It is necessary to multiply by prices in order to put different goods and services in the same dollar value. However, the nominal product cannot inform on the change in the number of goods and services over time since a change in the product can arise from both a change in the level of goods and a change in the price level. The real product, however, allows comparison. It reports the product using prices in a base year. Holding the price level constant, any change is indicative of a change in the level of goods and services.

Although the Department of Commerce considers diverse sources of income, it is unable to capture the total economy and therefore is also unable to

	1996	1997	1998
Gross domestic product (GDP)	3.4	3.9	3.9
Personal consumption expenditures	3.2	3.4	4.9
Durable goods	6.3	6.8	10.2
Nondurable goods	2.4	2.4	3.9
Services	3.0	3.2	4.3
Gross private domestic investment	8.8	11.3	10.3
Fixed investment	8.8	8.3	11.4
Nonresidential	9.3	10.7	11.8
Residential	7.4	2.5	10.4
Change in business inventories (CBI)	.....	.....	.....
Net exports of goods and services	.....	.....	.....
Exports	8.5	12.8	1.5
Goods	9.7	15.4	2.2
Services	5.6	6.6	-0.2
Imports	9.2	13.9	10.6
Goods	10.0	14.7	11.5
Services	5.4	9.9	5.8
Government consumption expenditures			
and gross investment	1.1	1.3	0.9
Federal	-1.1	-1.6	-1.0
National defense	-1.3	-3.2	-2.7
Nondefense	-0.5	1.7	2.4
State and local	2.4	3.1	2.0
Addenda:			
Gross national product (GNP)	3.4	3.7	3.7
Disposable personal income	2.8	2.8	3.2

Source: Bureau of Economic Analysis, http://www.bea.doc.gov/bea/newsrel/gdp299p.htm

Table 3 Excerpt from the NIPA. Real GDP and related measures; percentage change from preceding period.

growth in the long-term productive potential of the economy. Clearly, the former is less desirable than the latter. In addition, growth involves industrialization and the expansion of infrastructure such as roads and railways, which cause pollution, noise, the running down of natural resources, and environmental destruction. Many environmentalists argue that economic growth is not sustainable in the long run given that many of these resources are nonrenewable and given the limited capacity of the environment to absorb pollutants such as greenhouse gases, and toxic waste.

It is also important to recognize that a country's growth rate is not necessarily the same as the long-term steady-state output

level. Very often less-developed countries experience higher growth rates than more developed countries. For example, in 1988 India had a GDP 75 times as large as Sweden's while remaining substantially poorer. In these cases, given the country-specific factors—a large, unskilled population, for example, and a low stock of capital—it can expect its growth rate to diminish over time.

When the policymaker seeks to increase long-term output per head of the population, and thereby short-term growth, the only hope is to influence country-specific factors. These factors include the country's savings rate, rate of depreciation, the rate of population growth, and the rate of technological growth.

LEFT: If individuals work on their own land rather than hiring someone else on the open market to do the work for them, then this work may go unreported in the National Income accounts.

accurately measure economic well-being. The compiled data only include market activity; work done by housewives or people working on their own land, for example, has no price tag. The statistics also omit any value attributed to leisure, the ecological costs of pollution or garbage, and "bads" (such as consumer spending to replace possessions lost in a natural disaster) as well as "goods." Most specifically, the Department of Commerce cannot provide statistics on the underground economy. For example, when workers are paid in cash or receive tips, it is in their best interests to withhold information on that income in order to avoid taxation.

Similarly, work performed by illegal immigrants tends to go unreported. Perhaps the most notable example of the underground economy is the black market, where goods are bought and sold illegally. For example, during times of rationing, goods are sold on the black market for a higher price than dictated. Illegal goods—drugs, for example—and goods smuggled across borders to avoid paying taxes are also sold on the black market. Because these acts are illegal, they are not reported in the national income and product account. In fact, the national economy measures activity in organized markets and not national welfare.

Balance of Payments

The balance-of-payments account indicates the level of net exports—it is the amount of domestic goods leaving the country less the amount of foreign goods entering the country. In effect, it is a record of a country's trade with the rest of the world. In simple terms it is true to say that when the country has a balance-of-payments deficit, it imports more than it exports; similarly, when it experiences a balance-of-payments surplus, it exports more than it imports.

Government policymakers are often concerned when a country finds itself in a balance-of-payments deficit. Consistently importing more than exporting implies a lower level of aggregate demand for the country's goods. This serves to decrease the country's level of employment. With a deficit on the balance-of-payments account a country will have to sell assets such as foreign exchange, real estate, government bonds, or stocks to pay for the imports that exceed the value of exports. The country might eventually have to devalue its currency. Alternatively, to eliminate a balance-of-payments deficit, a country can block other countries' goods from entrance. Or it can increase tariffs, the taxes on imports, which in turn causes the prices for foreign goods to rise relative to those of domestic goods, thus making domestic goods more attractive and stimulating demand for them.

An introduction to the federal budget

ABOVE: The president's budget comprises all requests of the various federal agencies combined and then submitted to Congress.

Each year, the federal government publishes the budget of the United States, a document several hundred pages long. This budget has enormous power to influence growth and stagnation in the economy, employment and unemployment, inflation and deflation, and income redistribution via taxation and transfer payments.

The federal budget document gives expected federal receipts—money to be paid to the government in the form of income taxes, social insurance taxes, corporate and excise taxes, etc.—and proposed federal outlays—money to be paid out by the government on national defense, law and order, Social Security payments, net interest on the public debt, and so on—for the following year. For the budget to balance, federal receipts should be equivalent to federal outlays. The document also includes a collection of tables that summarize past budget information.

For most of the 20th century the United States saw a movement from a federal budget surplus—where receipts were greater than outlays—to a federal budget deficit—where receipts were less than outlays. This led to a gross federal debt (known as the national debt or the public debt) of close to 56 percent of GNP by the end of the 1980s. This debt is the money owed by the U.S. government to banks, institutions, investors, etc. However, after a period of several years of high growth, low unemployment and low inflation, 1999 saw the federal budget facing a surplus for the first time in 30 years.

The 20th century also saw movement toward a much greater role for federal, state, and local government in the

United States. So, for example, while total government outlays in 1929 were 10 percent of GNP, with government receipts 11 percent, by 1989 these figures had increased to outlays of some 32 percent of GNP and receipts of 30 percent. With around a third of the nation's GNP now being cleared through the government—that is, passing through federal, state, and local government hands—the United States has become very much a mixed economy.

History of the budget

From the beginning of the 19th century up until 1921, Congress was concerned with limiting central government power. As a result, federal agencies submitted individual budget requests directly to Congress; the president had no control over the size and composition of these requests, and had no authority to amend them.

Then the Budget and Accounting Act was passed in 1921, which established an executive budget. Since then the president (rather than individual federal departments) has submitted budget requests to Congress. All requests of the various federal agencies are combined, and this consolidated request has become known as the president's budget.

Later, the role and functions of the federal government (as compared to activities at the state and local level) were expanded. The most significant centralization of power first came about as a result of the New Deal, the government's policy response to the Great Depression in the 1930s. Power was even further moved to the center during the 1960s and 1970s.

With this expansion of the federal government role came a corresponding broadening of the budgetary role of the president.

Since the 1930s and the New Deal the allocation of resources among different federal programs has always involved Congress evaluating programs and their benefits in the light of what the president's objectives are in his budget; final decisions are made within the framework of what the president puts forward. Aspects of the president's budget can be (and often are) rejected by Congress, but the framework is never rejected completely.

The role of the state

According to Adam Smith, the role and functions of government should be limited to defending society, administering justice, maintaining good roads and communications, and providing for institutions of education and religious instruction. If the role of government in the United States were confined to these functions, it would only have to collect taxes enough to cover:

• Expenditure on national defense. That is, providing military personnel; the procurement, operation and maintenance of equipment; research and development; military construction, provision of housing, etc.

• The administration of justice. That is, federal law enforcement; federal police activities and litigation; administration of prisons, and so forth.

• Spending on education, including training and employment. That is, money paid out for elementary, secondary, and vocational training; money for higher education, for research, and for general educational aids.

• Expenditure on general government functions and administration. That is, providing for the legislative functions of government, for management at the center, central judicial operations,

general records and property management, fiscal management, and related activities.

The above activities of government in the United States actually accounted for around 38 percent of the total federal budget outlays in 1989 and just over 30 percent of budget outlays in 1995. Clearly, the modern role and functions of federal, state, and local government far exceed what was originally envisioned by Smith.

Within the above "core" functions the array and scope of activities have significantly expanded. There are also broad present-day government activities that are not included in the above. Many of them come under categories that might be termed "public welfare" and "economic development," along with net interest paid out by the government to service the national debt.

Public welfare mainly comprises provision for income security—that is, retirement and disability insurance, unemployment compensation, housing assistance, food and nutrition assistance, and so on.

Economic development provides support for critical economic activities. Examples include investment incentives for firms and businesses, research and development, business tax rebates, and subsidies for industrial policies. Expenditures on human capital—that is, money paid out on education and health—might also be included as part of this category.

Net interest must be paid out to those banks, institutions, and investors holding the national debt.

Additional outlays by government are also made to cover for the large regulatory role of government. This covers the administration of regulation agencies controlling monopolistic price fixing, abusive practices in banking and securities, protecting customers from unsafe products, and so on.

LEFT: The administration of justice has always been, and remains, an important function of government. Governments must collect enough taxes to cover this role and others.

Policy instruments

One of the earliest debates among economists is whether to use fiscal or monetary policy as an instrument to affect the economy. This is a case of choosing a governmental instrument in the circular income model (fiscal policy) or one in the money market (monetary policy).

The first, fiscal policy, uses taxation or government spending to induce economic activity. For example, the government might increase spending and reduce taxation to stimulate aggregate demand—people have more money in their pockets and so go out and buy more goods and services. Alternatively, the government might tighten fiscal policy, reducing public or government expenditure and increasing taxation to curb aggregate demand—if, for example, the economy appears to be heading toward the peak of a business cycle.

Monetary policy, on the other hand, uses the quantity of money in the economy, the exchange rate, or the interest rate to produce these effects. By targeting growth in the money supply, for example, the government aims to control aggregate demand and therefore inflation. Alternatively, the government might choose to adjust the nominal interest rate; moving it down, for example, will increase spending by firms on capital goods since the cost of borrowing is cheaper. The exchange rate for a country's currency might also be manipulated in monetary policy. Devaluing the currency, for example, will make that country's exports relatively cheap compared to foreign imports, hence stimulating domestic demand.

Public debt as a percentage of output

During the 1990s Congress has found itself in a debate over both the necessity to balance the budget and, in the event of a budget surplus, the need to repay debt. Arguably, the salience of the debate stems from the fact that debt has increased since the late 1970s. Although absolute levels may be higher than ever, the increase has yet to result in historically high rates of debt measured as a percentage of output. (Source for figure: Barro, Robert. *Macroeconomics*, 1993.)

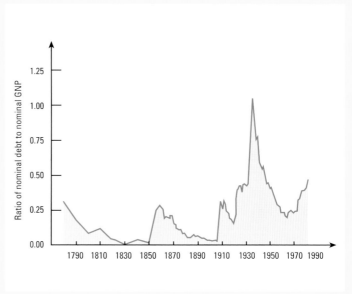

Figure 8 Public debt as a percentage of output ,1790-1990.

LEFT: *If a fiscal policy is pursued by the government, then it can either decrease taxation or increase expenditure on public goods and services; either way, this spending represents an injection of cash into the economy.*

Interest rates versus money

Alternatively, the policymaker might pursue a monetary policy, attempting to boost or prevent overheating in the economy via one of two instruments: adjusting the nominal interest rate, and hence investment spending by firms, or controlling the money supply, and hence the money-market equilibrium.

Once the instrument is chosen, the government must select the level of the instrument used. Assuming the government's goal is to minimize the cycles about the business cycle trend, neither choosing the nominal interest rate nor money balances is optimal. Instead, because the economy is faced with shocks to both the money-market equilibrium and the investment-spending equilibrium, it is optimal for the government to use a mixed instrument, selecting pegged interest rates. Setting the nominal interest rate serves to eliminate any effect of shocks on the economy. In contrast, setting the money supply forces the interest rate to rise or fall, and this partially offsets shocks to spending behavior. Using an instrument that allows both the money supply and the interest rate to adjust serves to minimize the disturbances by allowing both spending and portfolio disturbances to be mitigated.

Issues in fiscal policy

In attempting to implement fiscal policy, governments often find themselves in debate. Sometimes the debate is theoretical; at others it is more about real life situations.

The famous British economist David Ricardo suggested during the early part of the nineteenth century that it does not matter

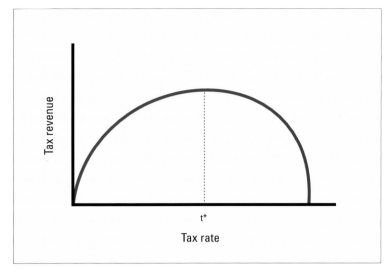

Figure 10 The Laffer curve.

whether the government increases taxes or goes into debt to pay for its expenditure. This view has been criticized because, it is claimed, when the government goes into debt, the future wealth of the economy is diminished.

Nor is choosing the level of taxation easy in theory or in practice. The goal of the government in setting the tax rate is to raise revenue. However, increasing the tax rate can at times result in a loss of revenue. This result was demonstrated by U.S. President Reagan's advisor, Arthur Laffer.

The Laffer curve, depicted in Figure 10, indicates the optimal tax rate when taxes are levied on income. If the tax rate is zero, the revenue raised is necessarily zero. As the tax rate rises, a higher percentage of income goes

BELOW: In the United States the central bank is called the Federal Reserve (often abbreviated to the Fed). Its headquarters are located in Washington D.C.

Since the 1970s the choice of instrument has been less of a concern than the ability of the government to influence the economy in the first place, because when the labor market clears and demand for labor equals supply, the equilibrium wage and employment level is achieved. In this case the aggregate supply curve is vertical; and as demonstrated in Figure 10, a shift in the aggregate demand curve will result in the same level of employment but a higher price level. In this section it is assumed that there are actually rigidities in the labor market, so that the real wage is above equilibrium, and employment is below equilibrium. As prices rise, the real wage is reduced, and employment rises; this results in an aggregate supply curve whose slope is positive. Therefore, when aggregate demand shifts outward, output increases. In this case government policy then can influence output.

As explained above, both fiscal and monetary policy can be used to shift out aggregate demand and, therefore, output. At the heart of the fiscalist-monetarist debate are the empirical estimates of how responsive the demand for money in the economy is to government policy.

Fiscalists believe that money demand is extremely responsive to the interest rate. A small decrease in the interest rate will make the cost of borrowing cheaper. This will increase the demand for cash by consumers and will increase output substantially. Therefore, should the government implement a fiscal expansion, boosting demand in the economy, output will increase by almost the same as the shift in government policy.

Monetarists, however, believe that money demand is relatively unresponsive to the interest rate. Therefore a decrease in the interest rate will not increase demand for money by very much. Expanding fiscal policy increases output by only a very small amount. According to monetarists, this means that expanding monetary policy is a more effective mechanism by which the economy can be stimulated.

So policymakers facing high levels of unemployment have a number of choices: fiscal policy—boosting aggregate demand via increased government spending or tax cuts—or monetarist policy—boosting economic activity via reducing interest rates or allowing the money supply to expand. Similarly, with high levels of inflation, policy decisions have to be made—cuts in government spending and tax increases, say, versus interest rate hikes and reducing the money supply.

Spending versus taxation

If the government decides to pursue a fiscalist initiative, it must decide how to bring it about. To boost the economy, the government can decrease taxation—cutting the rate of income tax, for example, or cutting corporate taxes so that consumers' incomes are effectively increased or firms have more income available for investment. Alternatively, the government can increase its expenditure on public goods and services such as policing, education, and healthcare programs. Apart from the wider benefits to the community, this spending represents an injection of cash into the economy and should boost aggregate demand in similar ways to taxation cuts.

ABOVE: If the government decides to spend money to stimulate aggregate demand, then people have more money in their pockets and so go out and buy goods and services.

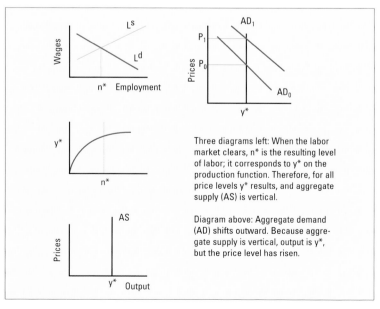

Three diagrams left: When the labor market clears, n* is the resulting level of labor; it corresponds to y* on the production function. Therefore, for all price levels y* results, and aggregate supply (AS) is vertical.

Diagram above: Aggregate demand (AD) shifts outward. Because aggregate supply is vertical, output is y*, but the price level has risen.

Figure 9 When AS is vertical, a shift in AD only serves to increase inflation.

23

to the government; therefore, tax revenue rises. At the same time, because the individual receives a smaller proportion of his or her income, he or she has incentive to work less and increase leisure. Eventually, the effect of individuals choosing to work less dominates the effect of the tax rate increase, and tax revenue begins to decline. There is an optimal rate of taxation that maximizes government revenue.

Issues in monetary policy

Monetary policy is set by the central bank. The central bank is not one where individuals deposit money. Instead, the central bank's customers are regular main street banks. Countries have requirements that force banks to deposit money in the central bank. This offers the central bank monopoly power in setting the money supply and the interest rate. The person in charge of the central bank is often referred to as the central banker.

Although the central bank is a separate entity from the government, in some countries the central bank exhibits more independence than others. If, for example, the central banker's job depends on approval of the politicians in office, the banker's independence is questionable.

In the United States the central bank is called the Federal Reserve (abbreviated to the Fed), and the central banker is the chairman of the Fed. The chairman is appointed by the president and approved by the Senate. His tenure in office is 14 years; the term cannot be renewed unless he has taken over another's term. The chairman cannot set monetary policy alone; instead, policy is set by the Federal Open Market Committee (FOMC). The FOMC is comprised of seven governors, including the chairman, who are similarly appointed; the five remaining members are state reserve bank members.

Economic policy in practice

To understand the many changes in economic activity, policymakers collect and study various data, or macroeconomic indicators—that is, measures of output, prices, and unemployment. All terms and definitions are specific to the United States, although many countries use similar indicators.

Measures of output

Output is measured by the Bureau of Economic Activity, Department of Commerce. These indicators are part of the National Income and Product Report (NIPR).

•Gross National Product (GNP) is a measure

of the market value of all final goods and services produced by U.S. residents in and outside the United States, and profits earned from firms owned by U.S. residents outside the U.S. during a specified period of time, normally a year. GNP was the leading indicator of national output; in 1992 the U.S. government followed other countries and began using the Gross Domestic Product as its leading indicator.

•Gross Domestic Product (GDP) is the market value of all final goods and services produced within the borders of the United States regardless of ownership.

•Net National Product (NNP) is the market value of goods and services produced by labor and property supplied by U.S. residents. By calculation it is output less capital depreciation. It is measured by computing the GNP less the Capital Consumption allowance (or gross investment net of that capital used up in the production of real output). GNP has gross investment, while NNP has net investment.

Measures of prices

The Consumer Price Index (CPI) is a measure of the price level. It indicates how various shocks to the economy, such as bad weather, affect the pocketbooks of the average household. The CPI is compiled by the Bureau of Labor Statistics (BLS); the CPI for the previous month is released about the middle of the current period. It is compiled by surveying the prices of a "basket" of goods that include over 300 typical items bought by households. The

ABOVE: Alan Greenspan, Chairman of the Federal Reserve, has presided over a period of almost unprecedented growth, low inflation, and high employment in the United States.

BLS sums up the prices of these goods after weighting the goods to their degree of use.

Recently, the BLS has implemented an experimental CPI that uses a geometric mean. The traditional CPI fixed weights to indicate the percentage of the good's use. In doing so, it fails to account for the fact that as the price of a good increases, people substitute away from it. Therefore, the weight cannot be fixed but must depend on the price level.

Measuring unemployment

The unemployment rate is measured by the Bureau of Labor Statistics (BLS). Figures for the previous month are released the first Friday of the month. To compile this data, the BLS surveys about 60,000 individuals to determine the rate of unemployment. This rate is the level of unemployed as a percentage of the total force.

The unemployment rate excludes a number of individuals. For instance, it does not include those not in the workforce, individuals who are either less than 16 years of age or above this age but are neither employed nor seeking employment. Therefore those who desire a job but are prevented from working due to family responsibility are considered out of the workforce. Similarly, discouraged workers, those who believe there are no jobs available and therefore do not seek employment, are not part of the workforce. Further, others are excluded due to measurement difficulties. The homeless are not included because the BLS conducts

the survey by phoning households; since the homeless do not have access to a home or a phone, they cannot be included.

Supply-side economics

Supply-side economics was popularized by the Reagan administration in the 1980s. Advocates argued that the government could not affect economic activity via the traditional Keynesian instrument, aggregate demand. Implicitly, they believed the aggregate supply curve is vertical. Therefore output can only be increased by a supply shock. Closely related to this was the notion that tax rates could be

ABOVE: In economic policy the Democrats generally prefer reducing unemployment. To their credit, their average mid-term growth rates are slightly higher than the Republicans.

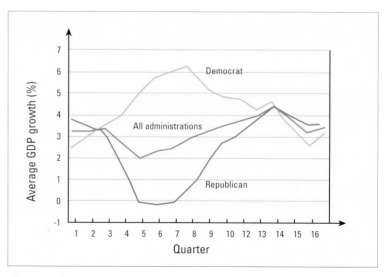

Figure 11 Average rates of GDP growth during different administrations.

26

decreased and still result in a tax-revenue increase. Ronald Reagan's economic advisor Arthur Laffer argued that the tax rates were so high that the revenue brought in by that level of tax actually exceeded the revenue lost due to a disincentive to work. However, this empirical observation has yet to be demonstrated for the United States. Preliminary estimates suggest the opposite: tax rates can be increased significantly without reducing revenue. It has been shown in Sweden, for example, that the tax rate that maximizes tax revenue is in the area of 70 percent. It was also found that the effect of the Reagan tax

cut on government revenue served to decrease receipts in all but the highest tax bracket.

U.S. party preferences

It is important to remember that some government goals are mutually exclusive—that is, the pursuit of one policy goal might preclude or work against the pursuit of another. So, for example, policies that tend to reduce unemployment and increase economic growth may cause inflation, and vice versa. Hence some kind of choice must be made by government.

The largest two political parties in the United States are the Republican Party and the Democratic Party. Although these parties consist of a widely diverse set of politicians, in general the Republicans are relatively more conservative than the Democrats, both politically and economically. They tend, therefore, to prioritize or choose different economic goals. So, for example, Republicans generally prefer decreasing inflation over reducing unemployment, while Democrats prefer increasing employment. Differences are particularly marked during an electoral campaign, with Republicans preferring to induce a lower rate of inflation, while Democrats offer lower unemployment rates. As Figure 11 demonstrates, the average growth rates are higher for Democrats than Republicans in the middle of their terms but even out toward the term end.

ABOVE: In general, the Republicans are convinced that decreasing inflation is the key to economic success. However, as an election approaches, growth rates of both parties tend to even out.

SEE ALSO:

- Volume 1, page 86: Inflation and deflation

- Volume 2, page 100: Market failure and externalities

- Volume 4, page 35: International trade and finance

- Volume 5, page 7: The business cycle

- Volume 5, page 40: Fiscal policy

- Volume 5, page 61: Macroeconomics

- Volume 5, page 71: Monetarism

- Volume 1, page 113: Unemployment

Government and the individual

The relationship between a government's economic policy and the individual citizen is one of the fundamental issues that economists address and is a critical area of political debate.

The relationship between government and the individual is of great importance to all citizens. In modern states free enterprise usually plays a central role in the relationship, and individual citizens generally have a certain amount of control over the policies of government through the democratic system. This has not always been the case. The relationship has changed radically through history and in states with totalitarian systems.

The economic relationship between a government and the people it governs is critical to both sides. It sparks intense debate for two reasons: first, because it is at the center of our view of how society should be organized; and second, because the way that government policies actually work in the real world is hard to define. What kind of impact does government policy, spending, taxation, and so on have on individuals? How do different policy choices affect the citizens who elect the governments—at least in a democratic society—in the first place? And what duty does the government owe to those citizens in terms of access to education and basic healthcare, access to housing, and a minimum standard of living? These are recurring questions.

Macroeconomic goals

Most economists agree that government has four broad macroeconomic goals: maintaining steady economic growth, keeping unemployment rates low, ensuring price stability, and—in the longer term—maintaining an overall balance on the current and capital accounts for its imports and exports. It is also agreed that the government should intervene in the economy to correct market failure and externalities, provide public goods, and—to a greater or lesser degree—redistribute income (*see* Government and the economy, page 6).

Even within this area of broad agreement there lie the seeds of conflict, however. Take the degree to which government fiscal and monetary policy can maintain full employment in the economy, for example, or keep

ABOVE: In line to buy coffee. Government regulation affects many parts of our lives, including tariffs on imports such as coffee from Latin America.

prices stable. Most economists agree that a tight monetary policy—controlling growth in the money supply by raising or lowering interest rates, for example—will go some way toward keeping inflation low. Most experts also agree that an expansionary fiscal policy, such as increased government spending, will go some way toward boosting employment. The situation is not that simple, however. The main policy objectives and priorities of whatever government is in power at any time will affect different sectors of society. Those living on welfare payments and those who are out of work will benefit if the government follows a policy of increased expenditure on public services, while those in high-paying jobs might prefer to see cuts in taxation and reduced government spending. Which sector does the government make its priority? Is there a sensible economic, rather than political, answer to the dilemma?

Such debates are not, of course, confined to economists and politicians. They are part of a debate within the community at large, and the self-interest of individuals in a democracy

plays an important role in determining policy. Politicians hoping to be elected have sometimes made promises about economic policies that were unwise and proved to have negative consequences. Governments in power hoping to be reelected have also tried to create a "feel-good" factor by spending more than might be wise at a particular point in the economic cycle. Political debate in democracies tends to magnify differences in economic policy between two parties, when in fact both often reflect a larger, often international trend in policy.

This chapter looks at the areas in which government policy affects the citizen: first, in terms of taxation, then, in terms of policies to control markets, and third, in the broader context of using economic policy to promote equality and to improve social conditions.

Taxes and spending

For most people taxation and direct government spending are the most obvious ways in which economic policy affects their lives (*see* Taxes, page 79). When governments intervene

BELOW: Public spending on healthcare and welfare for the less well off is an important part of the relationship between government and the individual.

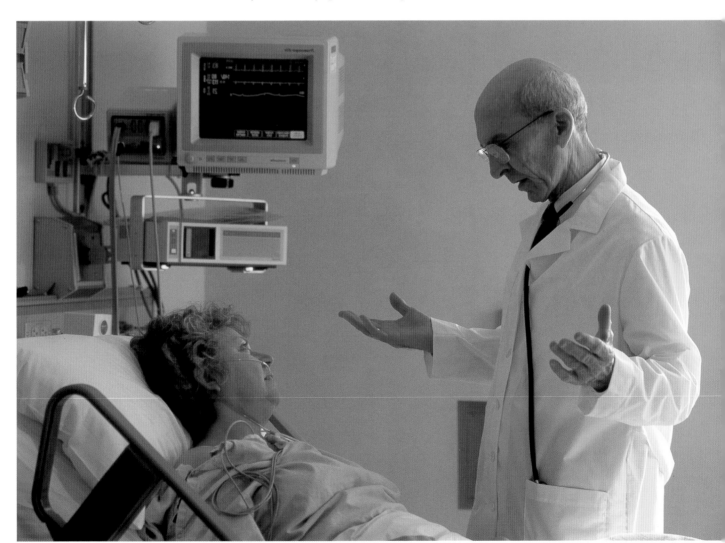

in an economy, they spend money, which they generate through taxes, to provide certain goods and services that are underprovided by the market. The people the government chooses to tax, the levels of taxation it sets, whether those taxes are direct or indirect, and so on will obviously have an effect on its citizens, as will the way in which the government spends the money it collects.

Many governments spend money in order to achieve a more equitable distribution of income in society, although the degree to which they do this varies enormously among nations and governments. Redistributive programs of this type may include the provision of social security systems, unemployment insurance, and welfare assistance.

In the United States the largest portion of federal taxes comes from levies on personal and corporate or business incomes. These taxes are progressive, meaning that individuals who earn higher incomes pay a higher proportion of their earnings in tax. However, income tax is not the only tax that U.S. citizens pay. Additional taxes are paid to the Social Security Administration and to state and local governments. A major source of revenue for state governments is sales tax levied on consumer products, while local governments and municipalities rely on income generated from property taxes.

Sales taxes

Many economists argue that the best taxes—by which they mean those that are easiest to collect and that cause least distortion in the economy—are sales taxes; they argue that income taxes or taxes on business profits

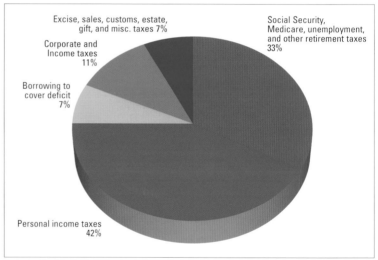

Figure 1 Source of federal taxes in 1997.

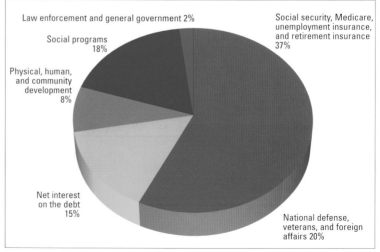

Figure 2 Allocation of federal taxes in 1997.

should be reduced wherever possible. Most governments, however, take the view that the tax system helps redistribute income and that this is a major function of government policy.

Once tax revenues have been collected, the government is faced with the difficult task of deciding how to spend the money. In 1997 the U.S. federal government spent 63 percent of the revenues it collected on projects with direct welfare benefits for citizens. For example, 37 percent of revenues were spent on the provision of Social Security benefits and Medicare—health insurance for elderly and disabled people—while a further 18 percent was spent on social programs. Another 8 percent was spent on physical, human, and community development. These last two categories encompass government spending on the provision of roads, schools, public parks, electricity, water, and social programs. In economic terms this spending was part of government efforts to compensate for market failures such as public goods and externalities.

It is important to note that the U.S. government spent 15 percent of its revenues on financing its debt. Governments go into debt when they do not have enough money to finance all the projects they want to implement. To overcome this shortfall in revenue, they may borrow money from international lending agencies such as the World Bank or the International Monetary Fund. These loans have to be paid back, along with any interest, and debt repayment accounts for a substantial portion of many nations' spending.

Market regulation

If taxes and direct spending are the most obvious cconnection between the individual and the government, government regulation of markets is less apparent but is the key to maintaining the health of the economy and protecting individuals as consumers. The neo-classical model proposes that the best possible social outcome results if there is perfect competition in all markets. In real world markets for goods and services, however, perfect competition, and even near-perfect competition, is rare. The existence of imperfect competition affects individual consumers and producers if resource allocation is not as efficient as it could be (*see* Government and business, page 43).

Imperfect competition occurs, for example, when there is only one seller or buyer of a particular good in the marketplace. The case of a single seller is known as a monopoly. Because there is only one seller of the good, that seller holds power over the price and becomes a price-setter rather than a price-taker. An example is the De Beers Diamond Company: as one of the few sellers of diamonds in the world, it is able to control the price of diamonds.

By charging higher prices, a monopoly may exclude some individuals in society from being able to purchase a particular good. Governments often step in and regulate the behavior of monopolies. They may force monopolies to charge lower prices for their goods, for example, in the public interest. Governments may also force monopolies to unbundle or deregulate. If a monopoly is unbundled, it effectively splits its operation into a number of smaller operations. Deregulation of a monopoly means that government actively encourages other firms to start producing the same good and become competitors in the market. To achieve this, government may offer incentives to the new firms, such as tax exemptions or subsidies.

Natural monopolies are a slightly different case. A natural monopoly occurs where the

BELOW: The workplace is often closely regulated by government in order to protect individuals in terms of wages and working conditions.

average cost of providing a service or a good is so high that it makes sense for one firm to spend all the money on infrastructure and outlay, and produce the good. If you consider the entire infrastructure that is required to pipe water or electricity to your home each day, it clearly represents a significant cost. It would not make sense for several firms to each incur this kind of cost. Instead, one firm assumes the entire cost and provides the service. Even natural monopolies are regulated by the government, however, to ensure that prices are not exorbitant.

Monopsony

Imperfect competition also occurs when there is a single buyer of goods and services, a situation known as a monopsony. A monopsony usually occurs in the labor market, where there may only be a single employer. Suppose there was a single factory in your local town that could provide employment for local inhabitants. Because the factory is the only employer in the area, it has the power to set wages at whatever level it likes. In all likelihood wage levels will be set quite low, since the employer would be aware of the fact that job-seekers in the town have very few other opportunities. In some cases wages could be set so low that workers are unable to support themselves or their families. To prevent this from occurring, the government has a duty to step in and regulate the behavior of the monopsony. In particular, the government

could pass minimum-wage legislation whereby it sets a minimum level that workers must be paid. This is a means of protecting workers against exploitative wage practices.

Providing public goods

It is also important for people that governments intervene in the economy to provide public goods, mixed goods, and merit goods. Whatever their political views, all governments allocate some of their spending to public goods: if they did not, there would be no national defense, for example, and no law and order. Most also try to make some provision for mixed and merit goods, paying for free or subsidized education, for example.

Public goods have the characteristics of being nonexcludable and nonrival in consumption. Nonexcludability means that it is not possible to exclude others from consuming that same good. Consider the beach or the public park: it is not possible to prevent people from using these facilities. Similarly, once a road has been provided, it is not possible to exclude some individuals from using it.

If a good is nonrival in consumption, it means that consumption by one individual does not reduce the quantity available for consumption by others. For example, if you visit the park, it does not mean that I cannot visit the park. We can both enjoy the park in its entirety. Simply because I drive my vehicle on the road does not prevent you from driving your vehicle on that same road. This is

BELOW LEFT & BELOW: Nonrival and rival goods. A beach is classified as a public good because all the population can use it. Hot dogs, on the other hand, are rival goods. Once one is bought and eaten, no one else can use it.

clearly different from a good such as a hot dog. If you eat a hot dog, I cannot eat that same hot dog. The hot dog is said to be rivaled in consumption.

Public goods also tend to be indivisible, and are consumed collectively. It is not possible to split them into pieces and sell them in the marketplace, so the market mechanism cannot operate properly. This is important because it is the market mechanism that signals, via the relationship between prices and demand, what consumers are prepared to pay for a particular good.

Free-riding

Price-setting by the market only works well if the benefits of consuming a good are available only to those who actually buy it. Suppose that the benefits of a good were available even to people who do not pay for it. Would you pay or would you try to "free-ride"? Take the example of street lighting. Suppose you live on a street with no street lighting. A private electricity firm comes to your neighborhood to investigate how much each household would be prepared to pay in order to get street lights. You know that once the street lights are installed, your household will benefit whether you pay or not, so your inclination may be to say that you are not willing to pay anything or only a small amount in the hope that everyone else in the neighborhood will foot the bill. This is called free-riding: you try to enjoy a service that is paid for by others.

The problem with free-riding is that every household in your neighborhood may think the same way you do; they will all underreport the amount they are willing to pay for the service. The electricity company, whose desire is to maximize its profits, may be disinclined to provide any service at all given such responses. The market would therefore underprovide the good. Because the market mechanism cannot price public goods properly, too few resources will be allocated to their provision, and the outcome will not be efficient. It is the role of the state to step in and provide public goods. Other examples of public goods include the judicial system, the police, the defense force, lighthouses, public parks, and free public transport.

Mixed goods

Government also supplies some goods that, while not strictly public goods, may have a public-good element. They are sometimes called mixed goods, examples of which include free education and healthcare. If education is provided universally and free of charge, it is nonexcludable. Nobody of an appropriate age can be excluded from

attending school. However, free education is not necessarily nonrival in consumption. The number of vacancies in schools is limited; and as each position is filled by one pupil, it reduces the availability of positions for others. In reality education and healthcare are not always provided free of charge. Where school fees or health premiums are charged, these costs may serve to exclude some individuals, especially the poorer members of society, from enjoying the services.

ABOVE: Schools are mixed goods and are usually provided by government.

BELOW: The Air and Space Museum in Washington, D.C., is an example of a merit good.

Providing merit goods

Merit goods are those whose consumption is deemed to be socially desirable irrespective of individual preferences. In other words, they are goods that we somehow think are worthwhile to society even though we ourselves may not personally wish to consume them. A good example is museums. While we might not all enjoy browsing through museums, most people would argue that they are a valuable part of society's culture and history, and should thus be provided. However, because there is a divergence between private preferences and social benefits, the market will underprovide these goods, thus necessitating a role for government to provide them. In effect, by subsidizing or providing these goods, the government undermines the notion of consumer sovereignty. It assumes the role of a wise, all-knowing agent that is better at determining what is in the best interests of its citizens than the citizens themselves.

In a similar vein demerit goods are those we think are detrimental to society and should be penalized in some way (through taxes or fees) even though we ourselves might personally wish to consume them. Consider alcohol and tobacco. These goods are subject to relatively high government taxation intended to discourage individuals from consuming them. Even though individuals in society may have a preference to smoke and drink alcohol, government ignores these preferences in order to bring about what it believes to be in the best interest of society's welfare.

ABOVE: Forbidding smoking in public places is an example of government trying to minimize a negative externality.

Externalities

An externality, also known as a spillover, occurs when transactions or exchanges take place outside the market, meaning that they are not captured by a price. The existence of externalities results in market failure and inefficiency in the economy; it also has a direct effect on individuals.

In pursuing their own self-interest, individuals make choices and take certain actions that hold consequences not only for themselves but also for others around them. The price individuals pay for a good reflects the satisfaction they receive from consuming it. However, their consumption of a good may affect others around them. The harm others suffer or the benefits they enjoy are not reflected in the price the individual has paid for that good. Thus the preferences expressed for a particular good are not an accurate measure of its value to society. The price mechanism fails, and the outcome is inefficient.

Positive externalities

Externalities may be positive or negative. A positive externality arises when the action of one individual confers a positive benefit on another individual, but the individual receiving the benefit makes no payment for the benefit he or she receives. For example, suppose your neighbor has a fierce watchdog,

LEFT: Positive externalities are associated with research and development. Unless government provides incentives to encourage investment, firms might underinvest in R&D and free-ride on the knowledge produced by others.

while you have none. Any prospective thief would think twice about breaking into your neighbor's house and your house too, because the dog would soon alert you to their presence. This is a benefit you enjoy as the result of your neighbor's actions, yet you make no payment for this benefit. The benefit you enjoy is not reflected in the price your neighbor paid for the dog or the money spent on caring for the animal. It is a positive externality. In theory, if the market mechanism were working properly, you, as the person enjoying the benefit, should be prepared to make a payment to your neighbor in return for the benefit he or she has provided to you.

While it may be difficult to see why the state would intervene in such a case, consider the example of research and development. Knowledge is cumulative, meaning that we all learn from the discoveries of those who have gone before us. Firms that engage in research and development use the knowledge of past discoveries in their own work. However, they are also aware that any discovery they make will be used by their competitors. These rivals will be able to benefit from the research without having invested a dime of their own. With this in mind firms may underinvest in research. Indeed, most firms might prefer to try and free-ride on the knowledge produced by others, attempting to capture the positive externality associated with another firm's research investment. To prevent firms from underinvesting in research, the state may intervene in the market and provide incentives to encourage investment. Furthermore, the state may legislate to protect the discoveries that firms make through the use of patents.

Negative externalities

A negative externality occurs when the action of one individual confers a negative consequence on another individual, but the individual suffering the negative consequence is not compensated in any way. Take the example of smoking. The choice individuals make to smoke holds consequences for their own health as well as that of those around them who inhale the smoke passively. Nonsmokers are not compensated for the negative consequence they suffer as the result of the smoker's actions. This is an inefficient outcome. In theory an efficient outcome could be reached if nonsmokers offered to make a payment to smokers to induce them not to smoke. Alternatively, smokers could offer to make a payment to the nonsmokers in return for being allowed to smoke. In reality, however, we rely on the state to intervene. Legislation has been passed in the United States that prohibits smoking in certain areas to minimize the negative impact on nonsmokers.

Negative externalities are most commonly associated with pollution. Consider the case of a factory that dumps its industrial waste into a river upstream. This confers a negative consequence on farmers downstream who use the same water for irrigation, anglers who catch

BELOW: Buying a used car is an area where many consumers are at risk because of adverse selection.

fish, or people who like to walk by the waterside. Usually no compensation occurs between polluters and those who suffer the effects of pollution, and the market mechanism fails to produce an efficient outcome. In recent years, however, the state has begun to step in and regulate polluter activities more closely in an attempt to make polluters internalize the costs they impose on others. For example, firms that have been identified as polluters may be required to buy pollution permits, which specify the amount of pollution they may emit on an annual basis. Alternatively, some firms have pollution taxes imposed on them that might be spent on cleaning up the pollution. Both these strategies raise the cost of polluting to polluters, which are forced to reconsider their actions and allocate their resources in a different way. Firms may even begin to devote more resources to pollution control.

Imperfect information

An important underlying assumption of the neoclassical model of perfect competition is the notion of perfect information, in which all consumers have all the knowledge they need to make choices in the market. Perfect information does not exist in society, and the result may be detrimental to both consumers and producers, so government may intervene to remedy the situation.

Information may be costly and is time-consuming to collect. Where information is lacking or asymmetric (one-sided), certain market transactions may not even occur. There are two main types of asymmetric information problems, adverse selection and moral hazard. Both problems are closely related to the fact that we live in a world of risk. Individuals, however, are risk averse—they do not like it—and so in everything they do people try to protect themselves from risk.

Adverse selection and the consumer

Adverse selection arises out of the tendency for the people who accept contracts to be those with private information that they plan to use to their own advantage and to the disadvantage of less-informed parties. There are many markets in which buyers use some sort of "average" statistic to judge the quality of the goods they might buy. Because buyers base their decision on this average, there is an incentive for some sellers to sell poor-quality goods in order to make a quick profit. Also, the price that buyers offer will be based on average quality. This means that sellers of good-quality products will feel that the price being offered is too low, and so they might leave the market. This could initiate a negative cycle of sellers leaving the market until the entire market disappears.

A popular example of how adverse selection might affect individuals is the market for second-hand cars. The sellers of second-hand cars have more information about the cars they are selling than the buyers. So, for example, someone selling a used car will know if it performs well for its model, age, and so on, or whether it is in fact in bad shape and liable to perform badly. The buyer, on the other hand, only has information about the car's type, age, and mileage: he or she cannot judge how the car will run. Given that buyers cannot tell how the specific car they are buying will perform, all cars of the same model, age, and mileage will sell for roughly the same price regardless of quality.

However, the price that buyers are prepared to pay for any car is reduced by the perceived risk of purchasing a wreck. This means that people with good-quality cars are less inclined to put them on the market because the market price will be lower than the value of the car they are selling. Traders with poor-quality cars are happy to sell at the low price.

ABOVE: *Road accidents, and their frequency, lead to problems for insurance companies, which are sometimes classified as being "moral hazard."*

36

This is an example of adverse selection. Those buying cars find it difficult to distinguish between good and bad risks, so they buy at a price based on an average statistic. This leads sellers of good-quality products to leave the market, which could lead to a cycle of falling quality and prices.

Adverse selection is also significant in the markets for insurance and credit, where there may be a significant imbalance between the knowledge held by buyers and sellers. In the case of insurance those who tend to buy insurance tend also to be the worst risks. Those selling insurance will find it difficult to distinguish between good and bad risks—between the safe car drivers, for example, and the poor drivers who are more likely to be involved in an accident. Again, the price insurance salespeople charge will be based on an average statistic somewhere between the good-risk and the bad-risk customers. This discourages those less at risk from buying insurance by making it expensive for them.

Moral hazard

Moral hazard is a different problem brought about by limited information concerning how an individual's behavior might change after a transaction has taken place. For example, an insurance seller does not have information about how a driver's attitudes or behavior might change once they have bought car insurance. It is possible that the driver might start to take more risks because he or she knows that should anything happen to the car, the insurance company will have to pay. The insurance sellers want to protect themselves from risk and in extreme cases might decide not to sell insurance to a particular driver. Exchange does not take place; the market does not work.

To overcome these information problems, government has a role to step in and try to improve information and make it more readily available to buyers and sellers alike. Government might also require that sellers provide a guarantee with their products. This will send a signal to buyers that the product is one of good quality. Government also requires that individuals obtain driving licenses. The license acts as a signal to the insurance seller that the individual does at least have basic driving skills and knows the rules of the road.

There are all sorts of incentive arrangements that can also help minimize problems of moral hazard. For example, insurance companies often require individuals to pay a deductible in certain circumstances. If you know that you will have to pay $300 in the event that your car is in an accident, you may drive more carefully. Government regulation

(in the form of licenses) and business policy (in the form of a deductible) work together to lessen moral hazard.

The broad debate

Government taxation and intervention in markets to make them work better are generally agreed to be good for individual citizens. However, the way that governments approach taxation and market intervention and the specific policies they use have to be put into a broader context. This broader context is the area of most heated debate among economists, both in terms of what is possible and what is desirable. In economic terms the question is concerned with what is called the equitable distribution of resources, or who gets the proceeds from what is produced.

The background to the debate is that almost all economists believe that general conditions in a society should be improved rather than worsened by economic policy.

BELOW: The unequal distribution of resources is epitomized here in Bombay, India, where slum huts stand in the shadow of comparatively wealthy housing.

Any society may include many poor people. Even where the market mechanism works well and economic output is growing, some people seem unable to obtain sufficient resources to sustain themselves or their families. How are their conditions to be improved?

There are two basic ways of answering the question. On the one hand, some people argue that government should only pursue strategies that will bring about economic growth. The benefits of this growth will eventually "trickle down" to all members of society. Other economists, on the other hand, argue that there is no guarantee that the benefits of economic growth will ever reach the poorer individuals in society and that, even if they do, it will take a long time. They thus emphasize that government should pursue positive strategies of redistribution in the economy, namely, transferring resources and incomes from the rich to the poor.

These issues are made very complex because it is clear that a relationship does exist between inequality and growth in an economy. Economists have spent a lot of time trying to understand the causes of growth and inequality and the links between the two phenomena. There are three major unresolved questions. First, is there really a "trickle-down" effect that will distribute the benefits of economic growth throughout society? Second, does positive government intervention to help the poor actually do the poor any good in the long term? The third, related, question is whether such government intervention on behalf of the poor might actually inhibit economic growth and therefore injure the economy as a whole.

The classical economists

The debate over equity for all individuals in a society—and how to achieve it—has persisted throughout the historic development of economics as an academic discipline. The classical economists were concerned with understanding how capital accumulation would occur, that is, how firms would save and later reinvest their profits in capital equipment such as machines, tools, and factories. This capital accumulation would stimulate growth.

In Adam Smith's view the best social outcome would be achieved by allowing the economy to function without any interference by government. David Ricardo, writing in 1817, built on Smith's ideas. He was interested in explaining why the total economic output, or Gross Domestic Product (GDP), was not shared equally by the different classes of a society.

His view was that this inequality in the distribution of output served to constrain economic growth. By dividing society into three classes, namely, workers, capitalists, and landlords, Ricardo argued that the profits always accrued to the landlords. Because they did not save, accumulation would not take place. To boost accumulation and stimulate economic growth, Ricardo advocated the redirection of the profit into the hands of the capitalist class. Unlike Adam Smith, Ricardo effectively emphasized the need for redistribution of wealth to occur via government action.

The Marxists

For Karl Marx, writing in the 19th century, the issue of equity was central to all economic analysis. Marx believed that capitalism was an inherently unjust system that perpetuated inequality through exploitation. He defined exploitation as the extraction of surplus labor by capitalists or producers. Surplus labor, according to Marx's definition, is the extra work employees put in over and above the value of their salary. He argued that the labor input into the production of a good or a service adds more value to that product than is actually paid for the labor that creates it.

Contrary to popular belief, however, Marx said very little about the role of government

LEFT: *Economic forecasters often influence politicians and policymakers. In an attempt to prevent the shortfall in benefits predicted for 2034, in 1999 President Bill Clinton announced plans to raise levels of U.S. Social Security.*

in the economy. In fact, economists of the Marxist tradition argue that the state is not always a clearly defined, even-handed institution. They take the view that it is more often biased toward those who control the means of production ("the rich") and discriminates against those that do not ("the poor"). This, according to them, explains why expenditures in many countries are skewed toward the urban rich. Thus, in Marxist terms governments, like the market, might fail to achieve the best social outcome.

Marx's ideas, as interpreted by Lenin, who took over power in what was then Russia in 1917, had an enormous influence on the new Soviet Union and also on the other communist states that came into being after 1945. In these planned economies relative equality of income was a crucial part of the relationship between the individual and the state. However, these totalitarian societies failed to compete with the economic growth of western societies. By 1989, when the communist states of Europe began adopting liberal economic policies, it was clear that the inhabitants of western states with higher levels of income equality were in general far better off than the citizens of former communist states.

The Keynesian revolution

It was the Englishman John Maynard Keynes (1883-1946), probably the 20th-century's most influential economist, who provided a sound economic theory to explain why government should play an important role in the free-market economy. Having lived through the aftermath of World War I (1914–1918) and seen the horrors of the 1929 Wall Street Crash and the ensuing Great Depression, Keynes concluded that markets clearly failed to provide the best social outcome in all cases. In his book *The General Theory of Employment, Interest, and Money*, published in 1936, he argued that governments should intervene to

ABOVE: Welfare spending on poor or disadvantaged children has been seen as an important government role since 1945.

play a stabilizing role in times of economic crisis and to stimulate the economy in periods of recession.

Although Keynes was not primarily concerned with the individual, his influence on state policy was noticeable. Extension of government action at the microeconomic level—that is, at the level concerned with individual consumers and producers—has been quite prolific since the end of World War II in 1945. In particular, government involvement in aiding vulnerable groups is now seen as inescapable. For example, many studies have found that poverty affects large families, the aged, and young children more than any other groups in society. Governments now give special attention to these groups.

Neoclassicism

Influential as Keynesianism was, during the 1980s neoclassical policies became very important within the United States and various European economies, including the United Kingdom. Neoclassical economics developed in the late 19th century. Neoclassical economists believe that any form of government intervention in the market is inherently inefficient unless the objective is specifically to correct market failure. For neoclassicists the only efficient way of doing things is to leave the allocation of all goods, services, resources, and so on to the market. Thus, in the neoclassical view telephone services, railroads, airliners, ports, and many other goods traditionally produced by the state can all benefit from being privatized. In other words, they argue that government-owned and -controlled enterprises should be sold to the private sector, which will result in greater efficiency.

A typical way in which neoclassical economic policies affect individuals is in welfare. Some neoclassical economists believe that welfare payments should be eliminated or substantially cut. This argument stems from a belief that by extending welfare benefits, governments make matters worse—that providing state assistance to poor households provides disincentives to work and thus prolongs unemployment. Reflecting this neoclassical consensus, Bill Clinton stated his intention to "end welfare as we know it" during his 1992 presidential campaign.

At the heart of the neoclassical argument over public action is the question of whether there are any tradeoffs between growth and inequality. The trickle-down hypothesis holds

BELOW: Should government or private insurance plans be the main provider of medical assistance to the sick? This is a major debate in modern society.

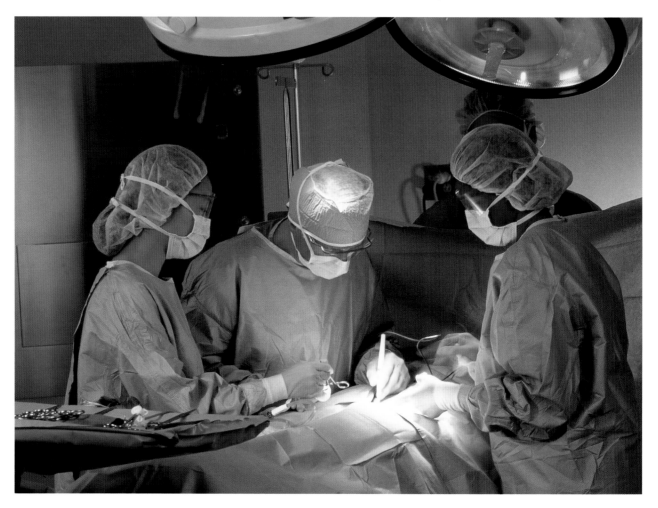

that if governments focus on increasing GDP, inequality will take care of itself as time goes by. This idea was first made explicit by Simon Kuznets in his seminal article "Economic Growth and Income Inequality," published in 1955. Kuznets undertook a systematic analysis of GDP growth patterns for several countries and observed that over time economic growth was associated with decreasing levels of inequality. Using this observation as a starting point, he constructed his "inverted-U" hypothesis. As growth proceeds, he argued that inequality would initially tend to rise. However, at some point the tradeoff will be reversed, and inequality will tend to fall as growth continues.

Refining Kuznets

Since Kuznets many economists have devoted a great deal of time to the empirical testing of the inverted-U hypothesis. The 1970s witnessed a proliferation of academic works supporting Kuznets's hypothesis as writers from different ideological backgrounds used his findings to triangulate their own positions. Some called for greater redistribution; others wanted to ignore the role of growth; a third group went to the opposite extreme of placing even greater emphasis on growth, ignoring the role of redistribution.

A further complicating factor in considering the relationship between growth and redistribution is that many economists have concluded that inequality is itself a major constraint on growth. If this were true, then it would suggest that social equality—which itself implies government redistribution of income—is an important precondition for economic growth.

Another group of economists is exemplified by Amartya Sen, a longtime critic of the trickle-down hypothesis and winner of the 1998 Nobel Prize for Economics. Sen argues that governments need to move beyond simply worrying about GDP. He suggests that while increasing GDP growth is important, more attention should be paid to whether or not growth leads to improvements in the quality of life for individual citizens. As Sen has argued, the process of economic development ultimately has to be concerned with what people can or cannot do—whether they can live for a long time, escape avoidable illness, be well nourished, be able to read and write and communicate, take part in literary and scientific pursuits, and so on. In this view economic development has to do, in Marx's words, with "replacing the domination of circumstances and chance over individuals by the domination or individuals over chance and circumstance."

The debate in action: social security plans

The economic debates about broad issues have vital relevance to the detailed relationship between government and the individual citizen in many ways. Take the example of Social Security. The basic aim of all social security programs is to provide a guaranteed income to especially vulnerable groups in society. In the United States they include the aged, families dependent on only one breadwinner as a result of death, and disabled individuals. Whatever is not paid out in benefits is reinvested in U.S. treasury bonds.

In President Bill Clinton's 1999 State of the Union address he announced plans to invest the budget surplus in order to enhance Social

ABOVE: Protestors at a demonstration in London, England, in 1999. The question of privatizing tasks that were formerly under the control of the state has provoked angry responses.

41

Security in the United States. The investment is necessary to prevent a future shortfall in Social Security by the year 2034, when it is predicted that more people will be claiming benefits than there are making contributions.

At the center of the debate is the whole question of redistribution, since Social Security is a form of redistribution through the fiscal system. In the United States the revenues generated from Social Security payments are regressive in nature, meaning that they affect lower-income groups more than higher-income groups. Since incomes are taxed only up to $72,600, those who earn more than this amount have to pay only the amount that applies to the maximum taxable income. Because of this asymmetry some economists have suggested that one way of making up the supposed shortfall that will arise by 2034 is by removing the income cap. This would make the Social Security tax progressive, so that richer people would effectively pay more social security taxes. This proposal has met with considerable resistance, especially from neoclassical economists, many of whom are advocates of privatization.

They have argued that it makes more sense to replace the current system with a system of private individual accounts that would be invested in the stock market.

Outcome of the debate

The outcome of this particular debate about government policy, based on opposing economic principles, will have important consequences for individuals. Neoclassicists argue that increasing progressive taxation will lessen economic growth and that everyone in the United States will be less well off as a consequence. Those opposed to this view argue that many people will find private accounts hard to manage and may be cheated by unscrupulous salesmen. Moreover, investing private accounts in the stock market makes everyone's pension vulnerable to a stock-market crash or a prolonged recession or depression. Which argument is correct, and how far should the government go in either direction? Economists and politicians would give a variety of answers, but the importance of the decision to each individual in society remains inescapable.

ABOVE: LEFT AND RIGHT: Is leaving the rich to spend their money as they wish the best way to ensure an equitable distribution of wealth in a society? Or does welfare encourage dependency and lead to a distorted economy?

SEE ALSO:

- Volume 2, page 100: Market failure and externalities

- Volume 5, page 34: Equality and equity

- Volume 5, page 81: Poverty

- Volume 5, page 89: The public sector

- Volume 5, page 116: Wealth

Government and business

The relationship between government and business is fascinating and almost infinitely complicated. They may not always get on politically, but economically it is inescapable that they need one another to survive.

Businesses need effective government in order to survive. Without laws, police forces, and courts to protect private property, for example, market economies would not be possible because it would be virtually impossible for people who accumulated profits to protect them from criminals. Many parts of the infrastructure that businesses use, such as roads and canals, are public goods—that is, they are amenities that are available to everyone and belong to no one in particular. Like individuals, therefore, businesses benefit from being provided with such infrastructure by government.

Mutual dependence

Governments for their part need businesses to stimulate economic activity within their countries, activity from which their populations will benefit. This is evident in many countries in the developing world whose governments are desperate to entice foreign firms to build factories and offices there, believing that economic activity will benefit the population as a whole. Increased economic activity stimulates demand, creates jobs and wealth, and therefore makes people happier. It also presents

more opportunity for tax-raising by governments, which tax business profits and receive more revenue from income taxes.

In creating or improving a successful society, a dynamic business sector has been seen as important by governments—for the last 500 years at least. Whether economic strength is seen to lie in a productive agricultural sector, a booming steel industry, or command of the world of new technology, governments and societies see business as being central to a nation's success.

From this mutual dependence it would seem natural that governments and business would get on well together and achieve a comfortable fit where government policies suited business and business operations suited government. However, this is far from having been, or being, the case. There are three principal reasons for this.

The nature of economics

The first reason lies in the very nature of economics. It is an imperfect science whose subject matter is infinitely complex; laboratory conditions do not exist, and it is impossible to come up with a single solution to any given

LEFT: Although the police and other agents of law enforcement are criticized in some quarters, their effectiveness is essential to the operation of business in a nation state.

economic problem. In the comparatively short period since 1945, for example, Western governments have had to consider Socialist or planned approaches to economic policy, Keynesianism, and classical and neoclassical theory. Socialism involves direct government control of key or even all industries and close direction of business, often with labor unions having a powerful voice. Keynesianism, named for the British economist J. M. Keynes, involves government regulation of demand in the economy through spending and tax policies. Classical and neoclassical approaches, meanwhile, involve using monetary policy to control problems such as inflation while government regulation of business is kept to a minimum.

Which of these economic policies has been the most successful has been the subject of great debate. Broadly Keynesian policies, often with socialist undertones, underpinned a long period of growth in Europe and the United States from 1945 to 1965. The defeated powers of Germany and Japan, for example, achieved great economic growth through the formation of a close partnership between government and all sides of industry.

The most successful economies since 1985, however, have probably been those of the United States and the United Kingdom. After the election of Margaret Thatcher as prime minister of the United Kingdom in 1979 and Ronald Reagan as U.S. president in 1980—both politicians who favored the free market and economic regulation through monetary policy—private businesses in both countries

were invited to undertake tasks previously performed by governments. In the U.S., for example, the government stopped trying to regulate markets such as domestic air travel.

Thus the boundary between government and private business is fluid. The degree to which governments regulate businesses, passing laws telling them how to act, varies greatly from time to time and from country to country. By the year 2000 a consensus had grown in the industrialized world that governments should not intervene in the economy except where necessary. Where necessity begins, however, remains the subject of debate.

The nature of government

The second complicating factor in the relationship between government and business lies in the nature of government. Not only do governments always have a number of economic policies to choose from, they also have pressures on them to behave in ways that are actually economically inefficient. In other words, although the smooth running of an economy may be a principal goal of government, it may often be overridden by other factors. During the 19th-century, for example, governments stopped or limited the use of child labor even though this increased the labor costs of factory owners and thus had an adverse effect on economic efficiency, because the social cost of exploited children was felt to be more important than business profits. Similarly, in the modern United States, the law dictates that businesses must pay workers at least the minimum wage.

LEFT: Under communism all foreign visitors to the USSR had to arrange their trips through the state-owned organization Intourist, which controlled all vacation packages and travel arrangements.

The nature of firms

The third reason why the relationship between government and business is as complicated as it is is because an individual firm does not necessarily have any interest in the greater good of the economy or the nation. By their nature businesses compete with each other for supplies and customers. The result of this competition may well create the perfect market that Adam Smith described, but any single business may want to destroy that market if it can by forming a monopoly in which it is the only supplier of a good or by creating an oligopoly in which it is part of a small number of suppliers from which new competitors are excluded. Sometimes the creation of monopolies and oligopolies may actually be encouraged by government; this is normally only under special circumstances, however (see below).

Governments have forces other than the purely economic acting on them, while an individual firm's interests are often opposed to those of the market as a whole. Hence the relationship between government and firms is normally complicated and sometimes antagonistic. As a result, there may be regular changes between competing economic policies. This chapter considers how modern Western governments have regulated business to protect markets and their citizens' wider interests; how business is regulated in order to create an effective legal framework; and how government legislation will also affect businesses, through legal liability, for example, bankruptcy laws, copyright laws, and patents. It also examines how the workings of politics and the political system itself affect businesses, and how business may influence government by becoming involved in politics; how governments encourage business; and how governments get money from business via taxation.

Markets and monopolies

If markets satisfy the conditions for perfect competition, governments cannot improve them. However, market failures—such as barriers to entry to a market, externalities, and imperfect information about product quality—mean that government regulation can improve markets. For example, it is possible that regulation could induce greater equality between marginal social and marginal private costs. Since, in the real world, all markets fail to a greater or lesser degree, many economists take the view that governments should play a substantial role in instructing businesses in what they can and should do. This role is not infallible, however. In certain circumstances government intervention may actually make markets worse.

Monopolies

A monopoly exists if there is only one seller of a particular good to a market. Often a firm is referred to as a monopoly if it controls say 80 or 90 percent of the market. In certain situations governments encourage a monopoly because it is felt to be economically efficient—in the case of a natural monopoly, for example (see below). In this way the U.S. Postal Service is the only company legally allowed to deliver first-class mail in the United States.

However, in general, monopolies are distrusted by governments and consumers alike. Like competitive firms, monopolies want to maximize their profits. Raising the market price might help them do this. Unlike competitive firms, however, monopolies and near-monopolies enjoy market power and can often raise the market price of their product without losing sales. In order to protect consumers against such price hikes, governments often act against monopolies.

ABOVE: *The monopoly formerly enjoyed by Standard Oil was the subject of trenchant criticism in the periodicals of the day, such as this caricature of John D. Rockefeller.*

Standard Oil

One of the most famous monopolies in U.S. business history was the Standard Oil Company of Ohio, created by John D. Rockefeller and his partners in January 1870. Rather than extracting crude oil from wells, they owned two refineries that turned crude oil into kerosene. To begin with, Standard Oil had only 10 percent of U.S. refining capacity. By 1878, after buying many more refineries, some of whose owners were forced to sell by Standard Oil's low prices, the company was refining 90 percent of U.S. oil. An antitrust case brought by the state of Ohio in 1892 forced Standard Oil to split into 92 smaller companies. In fact, however, the same owners kept control of all these subsidiaries, and in 1899 they were formally rejoined as the Standard Oil Company of New Jersey. In 1904 journalist Ida Tarbell published *The History of the Standard Oil Company*, criticizing the methods used by Rockefeller, and the company became the target of criticism from journalists and politicians.

Since it was refining most of U.S. oil, Standard Oil was evidently a monopoly. However, there was a need to split up the business only if it was the kind of monopoly whose market power caused high profits to the firm but a loss to society, rather than a natural monopoly, where one company dominated a business with high infrastructure costs.

Some economists have argued that refining was not a natural monopoly, and that since Standard Oil could not have prevented new refiners entering its market, it really had no market power. It was widely felt at the time, however, that Standard Oil used or threatened to use predatory prices. These are prices set below average costs in order to force rival firms out of the market. Backed by Rockefeller's huge wealth, Standard Oil would be able to survive a price war longer than other firms.

The breakup of Standard Oil

In 1890 the U.S. Congress passed the Sherman Antitrust Act, the first federal law against price-fixing and monopolies. A trust is a single large firm composed of many smaller ones; they were criticized in this period for raising prices and destroying competitors. Section One of the Sherman Act made illegal "Every contract… or conspiracy, in restraint of trade." Section Two declared "every person who shall monopolize… any part of the trade or commerce among the several States" guilty of a misdemeanor. The Justice Department brought a case under the act against Standard Oil in 1906. On May 15, 1911, the Supreme Court upheld a lower court's decision that Standard Oil had committed an offense under the Sherman Act and ordered it to be broken up into 35 separate companies. This took

ABOVE: In the late 19th century Standard Oil achieved such dominance in the U.S. market that it had no effective competition.

46

place on September 1, 1911, after which some of these subsidiaries went on to become Exxon, Mobil, and Amoco. Predatory pricing was then banned in the United States by the Clayton Antitrust Act of 1914.

Similarly, the Justice Department brought an antitrust case against the computer firm IBM in 1956. The federal government and 20 state governments brought a similar suit against Microsoft on May 18, 1998.

Natural monopolies

Where there are considerable infrastructure and setup costs necessary for the delivery of a good, a natural monopoly may occur. Examples include railroad tracks, electricity distribution grids, and gas, oil, and water pipelines. When potential competitors have no prospect of gaining entry to the market, profit-seeking natural monopolists would be free to restrict the quantities and raise the prices of the goods or services they are providing. Therefore governments often seek to regulate industries in which there are natural monopolies by, for example, telling them the prices they must set.

In the 1920s and 1930s U.S. airlines bid for government contracts to deliver mail. Policymakers worried, however, that no airline was profitable enough to develop successful passenger services. During the Depression the federal government was eager to make businesses confident that their investments would be profitable, and in 1938 Congress and President Franklin D. Roosevelt passed the Civil Aeronautics Act, creating the Civil Aeronautics Board (CAB). This board was empowered to control mergers between existing firms and the entry of new airlines into the market. It would also set prices and decide which airlines could fly on which routes. The Civil Aeronautics Act instructed the board to promote "competition to the extent necessary to assure the sound development of an air transportation system," a phrase which implies close state control of competition.

As a result of this legislation the U.S. airline business was closely regulated from 1938 to 1978 to avoid a natural monopoly and to ensure, it was claimed, orderly growth. Each airline was restricted to specific routes— United Air Lines flew north-south on the West Coast, while Delta and Eastern Air Lines flew in the same direction up and down the eastern seaboard.

Airline deregulation

By the 1970s high ticket prices had made the Civil Aeronautics Board unpopular, and government regulation was judged to have been a failure: people believed that there was insufficient competition in the number, quality, and costs of available services. In order to create a wider choice, government controls on quantity, price, and entry into the market were removed. The Airline Deregulation Act of 1978 withdrew the board's powers and allowed free competition among airlines.

BELOW: The growth and development of U.S. internal airline systems show the arguments for and against government control of business.

Many economists were optimistic that air travel would become a contestable market—one with few barriers to entry and many willing entrants. But no sooner had airlines been allowed to fly any route they wished than they created "hubs," central airports through which all their flights would pass. Airport hubs make flying to smaller destinations cheaper because airlines can run full planes between their hub and smaller towns rather than half-empty planes between two small towns. Since there is little need for more than one hub to serve the same collection of destinations, a hub network is a kind of natural monopoly. Small airlines have had difficulty in competing with the major airlines, which retain some market power. Hubs have enabled major airlines to reduce their costs substantially, though.

The deregulation of airlines has failed to produce a contestable market. Natural monopolies have reemerged in the airline industry, and with them have come the attendant internal efficiencies, bureaucracy, and market power. The history of the airline business may be used to argue both for and against government regulation, since neither has been particularly successful.

Regulation of pollution

Within an idealized, perfectly competitive market business activities should not affect parties other than the buyer and the seller. In reality, however, many economic activities by firms and businesses have "external" effects that affect bystanders as well as consumers and producers. Examples include the passive smoking smokers may inflict on others, the pollution of a river by a factory on its bank, or pollution of the air by motorists' tailpipes. Government intervention through taxation, controls, and legislation can reduce the effects of these externalities.

The potential inefficiency of markets that produce externalities—and the taxes through which governments could reduce the inefficiency—were first analyzed by economist A. C. Pigou in the early 20th century. Since Pigou's day more sophisticated policies have been developed, such as tradable pollution permits.

As an example of an externality, consider the market for flights leaving an airport near a residential area. The government can improve the market outcome because there is a particular failure in the market. Residents suffer constant noise, disturbance, and pollution from flights taking off and landing, but they are not compensated for the inconvenience. Private-sector remedies for the failure exist: local residents may, for example, pool their resources to buy the airport and then charge takeoff and landing fees. Most economists believe residents would have difficulty coordinating effectively, however, so that a government tax or a law saying what flights may take off and land remains necessary.

Efficient regulation of a polluting industry is difficult. In particular the government may not know what the efficient quantity of flights should be and therefore be unable to determine the correct tax rate to impose. Tradable

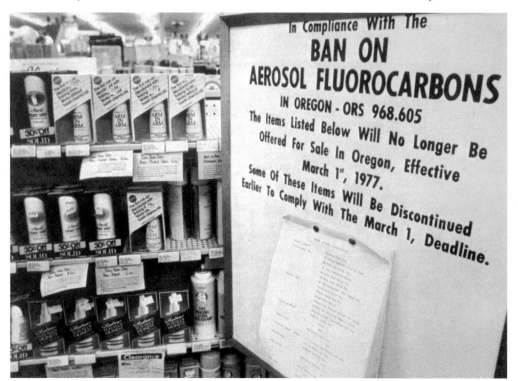

LEFT: Environmental concerns—most notably about potential damage to the ozone layer surrounding the earth's atmosphere—led to a ban on aerosol sprays and other emitters of chlorofluorocarbons (CFCs).

The *Exxon Valdez* disaster

ABOVE: A rescue tanker attempts to drain the holed Exxon Valdez *to prevent even more of its oil spilling into the sea.*

In March 1989 more than 500 square miles of the North Pacific Ocean and thousands of miles of Alaskan coastline were covered in oil after the heavily laden supertanker *Exxon Valdez* ran aground off Prince William Sound. More than a million barrels of crude oil were spilled, leaving slicks more than a foot deep on some beaches and thousands of dead birds, sea otters, and other wildlife. Huge claims for damages were filed against Exxon, the tanker's owner, by the State of Alaska and local fishing industries. Exxon was strongly criticized for doing too little too late and for failing adequately to staff the tanker or to supervise the crew. The company, meanwhile, blamed federal and state officials for cleanup delays. The trans-Alaska pipeline company Alyeska (of which Exxon was a leading member) was also charged with misrepresenting its ability to clean up an oil spill. It was described as "a sham behind which these partners have been hiding for the last 12 or 15 years." The lawsuit sought punitive damages, a negligence fine and money to restore the environment and the fishing industry.

This sad tale contains no moral but merely a question: Could the disaster have been averted if the U.S. government had exercised stricter controls over the "external" effects of oil tanker transportation, possibly by legislating to ensure adequate safety checks and imposing fines that adequately reflect the costs to the environment that result from such catastrophes?

permits to pollute, issued by the government but then bought and sold by firms, would help solve this problem. Higher demand by consumers for the goods or services of polluting industries, such as airlines, will raise the cost of the permits to the firms in those industries, thus increasing the price of emitting pollution. A market for permits would allow the cost of the permits to be set by market demand rather than by the government's estimate of what is appropriate.

The Environmental Protection Agency

The United States Environmental Protection Agency (EPA) was created on December 2, 1970. The Clean Air Act of 1970 and the Clean Water Act of 1972 gave the EPA considerable powers to regulate pollution. The first section of the Clean Water Act set out as a national goal that "the discharge of pollutants into the navigable waters be eliminated by 1985." Many environmental campaigners would approve of this goal of zero pollution, but it is unlikely to be socially efficient. To achieve a socially efficient outcome, the costs of regulating pollution—the costs to the polluting businesses—must equal the benefits to the environment and society of pollutants thereby being reduced.

Since 1970 the EPA has taxed many kinds of pollution and banned others, such as chlorofluorocarbons (CFCs) in aerosol sprays and foam packaging, which deplete the ozone layer. The EPA's actions have imposed large financial costs on businesses and consumers. However, it remains difficult to assess whether or not the benefits of the EPA's actions in terms of preventing damage to the environment or reducing the damage to people's health exceed the costs.

Adverse selection

Another type of market failure occurs when the seller knows more about the quality of the good than the buyer or vice versa. In such cases consumers become scared to buy because they are worried that they may end up with a worthless or dangerous product. Governments can lessen this fear by enforcing quality standards on business.

The imbalance or asymmetry of information that causes reluctance to purchase is known as adverse selection. One possible solution to the problem is for the government to establish an agency with the power to guarantee the quality of goods. In the United States one government agency that carries out this function on behalf of consumers is the Food and Drug Administration (FDA), now one of the most important regulatory agencies in the country.

The Jungle by Upton Sinclair

The Pure Food and Drugs Act of 1906 prohibited interstate commerce in adulterated or misbranded food and drugs. The legislation was a response to popular disgust at the description of poor hygiene and the processing of bad meat in Chicago meatpacking yards in Upton Sinclair's 1906 novel *The Jungle*. At first the Department of Agriculture enforced the 1906 Act, but in 1930 their policy was concentrated in the newly established FDA.

When it was first passed into law, the Pure Food Act was used mainly to maintain food standards; but with the development of new and powerful drugs since World War II the FDA has become closely involved in the drug and medical industries. Pharmaceutical companies must now get the FDA's approval before they can test a drug on humans. Then they must wait for the FDA to approve that the drug is safe and efficacious for the stated purpose before marketing it. Should the manufacturers wish to make a new claim about the drug, they must get separate approval for it. Since FDA regulation of which drugs can be sold reduces risks to consumers and reassures them, the market for pharmaceuticals may be expected to function better with this additional information.

Is the FDA efficient?

The process of FDA regulation is held by some critics to be inefficient or even unnecessary. Advocates for AIDS sufferers, for example, have argued that individual patients rather than a government agency should decide whether the risks attached to new drugs are acceptable. In 1988 pressure from AIDS victims made the FDA speed up its approval of drugs that might treat this and

other life-threatening illnesses. Critics of the FDA have also argued that private firms, concerned about the reputation of their brands, would act to prove their quality and safety even without the FDA's compulsion. This might be true in the case of the Coca-Cola Corporation, for example, which has a very valuable reputation to protect, but self-regulation would be less likely to protect the consumer from bad practices by smaller companies. The Food and Drug Administration, though sometimes controversial, will probably always be necessary.

ABOVE: One of the millions of birds injured by oil spillage from Exxon Valdez. The U.S. government is heavily committed to preventing environmental disasters of this type.

Merit and demerit goods

A further important way in which governments interfere in markets is by controlling demerit goods. They are goods that are considered socially undesirable regardless of consumer demand. Examples include alcohol, tobacco, and nonprescription drugs. In the case of drugs most governments consider that it is not desirable for people to be consuming any at all. In such cases governments may therefore intervene in private-sector market provision by firms and businesses to forbid goods entirely or to reduce the amount produced and demanded.

This may be done through the imposition of taxes, as in the case of cigarettes. Alternatively, the provision of demerit goods might be made illegal, as is the case with drugs such as cannabis, cocaine, and heroin. Making the production and consumption of a good illegal will seldom have the effect of reducing demand to zero, however; where there is demand, there will always be people willing to supply that demand. At the same time, government restrictions on the market may have undesirable side effects (see box, page 56).

Merit goods

A merit good is a good that is considered socially desirable regardless of consumer demand for it. Governments may intervene in the private sector in order to encourage the provision of goods of this type. The most common example of a merit good is education, which tends to be subsidized to a greater or lesser extent in most countries. An increasing trend in this area, however, is, for some governments to enter into partnership with private-sector businesses to fund the provision of these goods. Public-private partnerships of this kind are seen by many governments as a possible solution to the crises in funding that affect businesses for which subsidies are seen as important and necessary but for which public money is simply not available (see box, page 57). A similar example is the provision of public museums.

Legal restrictions on business

Governments affect businesses and firms in ways other than through regulation of markets and guaranteeing the quality of certain products. More general business legislation will also have an impact. It might include the ways in which different types of firms are incorporated. Bankruptcy laws, keeping accurate records, the way that businesses are required to treat their workers, and the legal status of trademarks, patents, and copyrights also have a practical effect on business.

Legal forms of businesses

Governments create strict legal definitions for business so that in business as a whole individuals and organizations know precisely where they stand if things go wrong. Businesses can be created and legally regis-

tered in one of several different forms. Each one involves very specific requirements in terms of how a company can be run and how much of its affairs must be available for inspection, for example, by registered auditors who examine its activities and report on them each year. The range of businesses has developed over the past 200 years according to what was felt to be efficient and simple to regulate. The three most important forms of business in the United States are the proprietorship, the partnership, and the corporation.

Proprietorships are businesses owned by one person. They are the most common form of business in the United States by number, though most of them are very small in size. If the firm cannot pay its debts or perhaps is sued by its creditors (the people to whom it owes money), the proprietor is held to be "liable" for all the firm's losses. In practice, if a proprietor is liable for debts larger than all his or her wealth, he or she goes to court and asks to be declared bankrupt. The bankruptcy

ABOVE: Butchers and other purveyors of foodstuffs are particularly closely scrutinized by government watchdog agencies.

51

ABOVE: U.S. Senate hearings on the drug thalidomide began in Washington, D.C., in 1967. The first witness to give evidence was Dr. Helen Taussing, professor of pediatrics at Johns Hopkins University.

court then allows the proprietor to keep a few assets so that they still have somewhere to sleep. The court also cancels any outstanding debts so that the proprietor can make a fresh start in life.

Partnerships are firms owned by a small number of people who are all "partners" in the business. The partners also typically run and manage their firm. Partnerships are similar to proprietorships in that although the partners receive any profits their business makes, they are also each liable for every debt the firm incurs. This is sometimes known as "unlimited liability," since partners have to pay debts of any size. Partners' unlimited liability might be seen as an advantage, however, in that they may have an easier time in persuading a bank to lend them money if the bank knows that each partner has every incentive to make the business succeed.

Corporate life

Corporations are the largest and most sophisticated forms of businesses. A corporation is owned by its shareholders, who receive any profit that the firm makes. Each share entitles its owner to cast a vote on how the corporation should be run. The shareholders may run the firm on a day-to-day basis, as partners do, or they may be people with little connection to the firm.

For example, as of November 1999 some 15.3% of the Microsoft Corporation was owned by its former chairman and chief executive officer, Bill Gates, who has a great deal to do with running the business. However, many other people all over the world also own shares in Microsoft, since shares in corporations may be bought and sold on stock markets. Most of these people have nothing to do with the day-to-day management of the corporation; their involvement with business decisions may be limited to an annual shareholders' meeting.

Often corporations are run by managers who are not themselves shareholders but who try to maximize the profits that shareholders receive. Shareholders can fire managers if they feel they are not doing a good job of running the corporation. A big difference between corporations and partnerships is that shareholders in corporations enjoy "limited liability." If the corporation goes bankrupt, the value of the shares will fall to nearly zero in price, but the shareholders are not responsible for having to pay off the firm's outstanding debts. They may lose the entire value of their shares but no more than that.

Bankruptcy

Individuals and businesses can be declared bankrupt in a bankruptcy court. Although people who own and run businesses hope that their firms do not go bankrupt, it is important for them to understand what would happen should they do so. The consequences of a business failing are the concern of much government regulation.

A firm that goes bankrupt typically owns some assets that still have some limited value. For example, an Internet firm may not be able to pay its debts, but it may still own its computers, telephones, buildings, and vehicles. When a firm goes bankrupt, all its assets become the property of its creditors. The creditors typically have to liquidate the firm's assets, or sell them for cash, to try to recover some of the money they are owed. People who own shares in the firm have no rights to these assets however.

The U.S. Bankruptcy Reform Act

Laws instituted by governments are needed to regulate the process by which a bankrupt firm's creditors attempt to recover their money. Typically, selling all the assets would not raise enough cash to pay back all these loan- and bond-holders, so agreement has to be reached on how the proceeds are to be divided up.

In the United States bankruptcy is regulated by the Bankruptcy Reform Act of 1978, which is often referred to as the "bankruptcy code." Under the code bankruptcies can be handled in different ways. A firm declared bankrupt under Chapter Seven of the bankruptcy code, for example, usually has its

BELOW: The stock from bankrupt firms is often sold at discount prices at auctions to raise money for creditors.

assets swiftly liquidated to pay back its creditors. A firm declared bankrupt under Chapter 11, however, will not have its assets sold but will instead be reorganized.

For example, a bankrupt Internet firm may have a well-known product, intelligent and skilled employees, and contracts with other firms. This could make it more valuable if it sold as a "going concern"—that is, as an operating business—than it would be if all its assets were sold off.

In a Chapter 11 bankruptcy the firm's creditors usually appoint a company of business experts try to keep the business running, perhaps closing down some of its operations and changing others in the hope that it will eventually recover and thereby be able to pay off its debts in full.

Labor relations

Another important legal consideration lies in the way that governments require businesses to treat their workers. Here again, strict economic criteria may be overridden by political or social considerations. Government attitudes toward the rights of workers have undergone great changes over the past century. In the late 19th century governments tended to discourage labor unions. It was felt that the power they gained by collective bargaining, or talking for a whole group of workers, in their campaigns for improved working conditions and higher wages interfered with the smooth running of business.

In the 20th century, however, labor unions generally became protected by governments. Similarly, the rights of employees to a minimum wage and to safe, healthy working conditions have become enshrined in law, often against the wishes of business leaders. In recent decades legislation has also made it illegal to discriminate against employees on grounds of race or sex. These are restrictions on the free operations of business but were felt to bring wider social benefit (*see* Government and labor, page 61).

Trademark, copyright, and patent law

A further restriction on business activities— but one that is acknowledged as being essential by most businesses—is that all firms must be careful not to infringe other individuals' or firms' trademarks, copyright, or patents. This is a method of protecting and encouraging innovation. Any firm that sells a product or invents some new product or process will also want to make sure that others do not use its name on their goods or use their invention without first paying to do so.

Trademarks are defined in the United States as names, words, or symbols that identify one firm's goods and distinguish them

ABOVE: Harrods, one of the leading department stores in London, England, has vigorously defended itself against attempts by various smaller companies to pass off its world-famous name and logo.

from those made by other firms. They include symbols such as the Coca-Cola logo or product names such as Jell-O. Although one firm can sue another for using its trademark even if it has not first registered this trademark with the United States Patent and Trademark Office, a part of the federal government, the firm is much more likely to win its case if it has previously registered the trademark. The Patent and Trademark Office (or PTO) will agree to register a trademark only if the mark is distinctive and unlikely to cause confusion with existing trademarks. For example, the PTO will not allow anyone to register "Coka-Cola" as a trademark because such a name would clearly be an attempt to claim association, or what is known to lawyers as "passing off." The PTO will also refuse to register descriptive trademarks like "cool refreshing drink," because they would serve more to confuse consumers than to distinguish one firm's products from another's.

Copyright is the right of ownership to original works, which may be books, articles, plays, songs, or films, but could also be clothing designs or computer programs. Copyright protects the "expression" of an idea, not the idea itself. Thus a songwriter cannot claim copyright for the idea of a song about being in high school, though he or she can claim copyright for the particular tune and words they have created to express this idea. Like trademarks, copyright for a work such as a film script may be defended in court even if the work has not previously been registered with the U.S. Copyright Office. As in the case of trademarks, however, authors are much more likely to win their case in court if they have first registered the script by sending the Copyright Office one or more copies of the script. Copyright usually lasts for the lifetime of the author plus 50 years.

Patents give the owners of inventions the right to exclude others from making or using their invention. This means that any firm that wants to use an invention must pay the inventor for the privilege of doing so. Designers can patent their creations, and more recently it has also become possible to patent plants, genes, cells, and even animals that have been substantially created in laboratories (although many people are uncomfortable with the idea that anyone can patent living organisms). To acquire protective rights over their inventions, inventors must apply to the U.S. Patent and Trademark Office (PTO). The PTO will grant patent rights only to inventions that involve a "nonobvious" improvement to existing inventions. In other words, an inventor must have come up with a truly original idea rather than simply adapting something that is already common practice. U.S. patents last only for a term of 20 years—after that time anyone can use or produce the invention for free.

Business and politics

Business naturally tries to influence government in its favor. Sometimes it does this through organizations such as chambers of commerce that lobby and make representations to government agencies over specific issues. Businesses are often accused of buying political influence through donations to the election campaign funds of their preferred candidates. If these politicians are elected and then keep prices artificially high in the industry in which those businesses operate, perhaps

by passing laws that make it difficult for new firms to enter a market, then shareholders and workers in the businesses that made the donations will benefit. Consumers, however, will suffer a disadvantage because of higher prices, and the overall efficiency of the economy will be reduced.

The amount of success that U.S. businesses have had in getting legislation passed that is helpful to them often depends on the degree of their influence with powerful members of the House of Representatives and Senate. Representatives or senators will recognize that what is good for certain firms is good for their district and will therefore vote in favor of the business.

Congressmen and women often try to get posts such as committee chairmanships that will help them protect businesses in their home states. Political reforms—such as greater control by the national parties of who chairs which Congressional committee—have

BELOW: The government of Alabama offered substantial incentives to Mercedes Benz to encourage the German corporation to build an automobile factory in the state.

Prohibition

ABOVE: During Prohibition, U.S. police zealously enforced the laws against the manufacture and sale of alcohol.

From time to time a government may attempt to regulate or proscribe certain goods or services if it feels that their availability would be detrimental to its people. In every society some people are strongly opposed to alcohol. In the United States in the early 20th century the antiliquor lobby became so influential that for a lengthy period alcohol was made illegal not just by the National Prohibition Act, which became law on October 28, 1919, but also by the Eighteenth Amendment to the U.S. Constitution.

Although Prohibition was strictly enforced, it did not stop the sale and consumption of alcohol—it merely drove them underground. There was a new crime, bootlegging (the transportation of liquor), and new clandestine drinking parlors, known as speakeasies. Alcohol became less readily available than before and harder to manufacture and distribute because of the danger of discovery by the police. These factors combined to force up the price of liquor, with the result that although the rich could still afford it, the poor could not.

Another point of interest to economists about Prohibition is that the period is a model of the establishment of a semimonopoly. For as long as it had been legal to drink alcohol, liquor had been manufactured and retailed by a wide range of firms and individuals. Now that alcohol was illegal but still in demand, the business fell into the hands of the underworld. The stronger gangsters drove out the weaker until there were only two big players left—Al Capone and Bugs Moran. Many economists believe that by the time of the St. Valentine's Day Massacre on February 14, 1929, when Capone's gang shot to death seven Moran hoods, the bootlegging market had already settled down, and the gang wars were fast coming to their natural close.

It soon became apparent that the legislation was unworkable, and by the early 1930s the Democratic Party had started calling for an end to Prohibition. Franklin D. Roosevelt's victory in the presidential election of 1932 sounded the death knell of the Eighteenth Amendment, which was repealed in 1933.

Schools out for business

In the United States in 1997 children between four and 12 years old spent an estimated $14 billion, and the total amount is currently increasing every year. Firms want to get as big a slice of this market as possible, and they have found an exciting—if rather controversial—way into it by sponsoring cash-strapped public schools.

U.S. schools that have taken up bigtime corporate sponsorship now have their hallways festooned with signs for national brands and local companies, computers with ad-bearing mouse pads, and basketball gyms decorated with logo-bearing banners.

Under an exclusive contract with Coca-Cola signed in 1997, Colorado Springs School District 11 will receive at least $8.4 million over 10 years—more if it breaks its sales target of 70,000 cases of Coke products a year. To help achieve these goals, staff have been urged to place vending machines in positions where they are accessible all day, and teachers are encouraged to let students drink Coke in the classroom. Other products have also been brought in: first prize in one of the school's Coke-sponsored contests—for a senior with a perfect attendance record—was a Chevrolet Cavalier automobile.

Coca-Cola is by no means the only company involved in initiatives of this type—some math books for third-graders contain exercises in which children are tasked to count Tootsie Rolls. TV station Channel One has become a leading supplier of free televisions to schools, along with advertising.

Many people have serious misgivings about the ethics of this form of sponsorship, which puts critics in mind of the Jesuits' claim that if they get children by the age of 7, they have got them for life. But impoverished public schools find it hard to resist corporate advertising when in return they are getting free computers or even free new football stadiums. In 1989 Colorado Springs School District 11 was $12 million in the red mainly

ABOVE: Although large firms are willing to pump money into schools, it is feared that these investments may engender brand loyalty in young people.

because the education budget had not been increased for more than two decades. Apologists for the district say that it has had to become more creative and businesslike in response to the challenge from the local taxpayers.

---

been proposed in a move intended to force Congress to act more in the national interest and less in the interests of locally important businesses. Events such as the failure of the McCain Bill (*see* box, page 59) have led many people to call for laws restricting the amounts of money politicians can spend on their election campaigns.

Without such laws many people fear that large businesses will always be able to use their money to influence politicians to make decisions that are good for shareholders but bad for workers or consumers and the overall health of the national economy. Other people argue, however, that such restrictions on campaign spending would restrict candidates' freedom of speech and dangerously limit the amount of information that is given to voters through broadcasts and advertisements.

Government purchasing power

The debates about local interests are just one level of the intermingling of politics and busi-

ness. Another is created by the purchasing power of government. Governments are usually the largest single purchasers in the economy. They are the biggest, and sometimes the sole, buyers of weapons, for example. On other levels, too, such as the purchase of computer systems or even pencils, a government may be a country's biggest single consumer. This has various ramifications. On the one hand, there is encouragement for businesses to use corruption to win big government contracts: this is a serious problem in many countries. On the other hand, government may have enormous influence in industries such as aerospace and may effectively control them through the allocation of contracts.

The level of business influence on government and the methods used to secure it can vary enormously from nation to nation. In some countries a culture of bribery has become accepted business practice. Western nations have strict rules about the amount of gifts or money that can be accepted by politi-

cians and for what purpose, but there is a fine line between a culture in which business is encouraged and has good close relations with politicians and one in which corruption becomes pervasive and leads to market distortions. Controlling business influence on government is a continuing problem.

Encouraging and protecting business

A major element in the relation between government and business is the way that governments encourage business. At its most basic this takes the form of ensuring that markets work efficiently. However, governments may also feel the need to interfere further and even to work against free-market forces. This often happens when a government feels that an industry important to the well-being of a nation needs to be protected against foreign competition. A classic example in the modern

world is the way in which the European Community protects its agriculture against competition from U.S. products by giving its farmers subsidies and erecting tariffs against agricultural goods from outside the Community. In Europe, especially in France, a thriving agriculture is felt to be part of the nation's identity, and so the residents of the European Community are forced to pay more for agricultural products than they should.

The U.S. steel industry

Meanwhile the steel industry provides an example of U.S. business lobbying that is bad for the U.S. economy overall. The U.S. steel industry was very large in 1950, but since then it has become apparent that other countries, such as Japan and South Korea, can make steel more cheaply. In 1999 the U.S. Congress voted for tariffs (or taxes) to be imposed on imported steel that was judged to be "unfairly" low in price. This tax on imports raised the price of steel inside the United States to the

ABOVE: *Since the end of the Korean War in 1953 South Korea has become one of the United States' most serious economic competitors, especially in the steel industry.*

58

How business interests affect legislation

Restrictions may be imposed on imports in order to protect the interests of a domestic industry. During the 1950s, for example, the two most powerful members of Congress, the House Speaker Sam Rayburn and Senate Majority Leader Lyndon B. Johnson, were both from oil-rich Texas. Their influence was important in the passage through Congress of restrictions on oil imports. One effect of these regulations was to raise the price received by American oil producers.

Also, during arguments over the 1981 budget David Stockman, director of the Office of Management and Budget, realized he could not persuade Congress to reduce subsidies to a nuclear power plant at Clinch River, Tennessee, because the majority leader in the Senate, James Baker, was from Tennessee. Stockman explained, "It just wasn't worth fighting. This package will go nowhere without Baker, and Clinch River is just life and death to Baker. A very poor reason, I know."
(Quoted in "The Education of David Stockman," article by William Greider, The Atlantic Monthly, *December 1981.)*

Another case occurred in the late 1990s, when a number of politicians and journalists argued that tobacco companies exerted an unhealthy influence on Congress because they were major contributors to the reelection funds of many Congressmen and women from both parties. Tobacco and other companies also hire lobbying firms in Washington, D.C., to attempt to persuade Congressmen and their staffs to vote for or against a particular bill. Companies may also spend money on advertising, telling voters that a law would not be in their interests.

In 1998 Senator John McCain sponsored a bill that would have added $1.10 in tax to the price of a packet of cigarettes. Tobacco companies spent $50 million on television advertising criticizing the McCain Bill. Senator Christopher Bond of Missouri reported receiving 400 calls from voters supporting the bill and 50,000 calls against it. Senator Bond voted against the McCain Bill, and Congress did not pass it.
(Extracted from an article by Major Garrett in U.S. News, *June 29, 1998.)*

benefit of shareholders and workers in the steel companies but to the cost of American construction companies and other purchasers of steel. Here again, political considerations override sound economics. Politicians often feel they must support steelworkers, who are well organized and vocal in expressing their interests, and they are also aware that steel is one of the key modern materials. As the greatest political power on earth, the United States feels it must maintain a large steel industry.

Similarly governments often wish to protect young industries by preventing competition from abroad. The Japanese government was widely felt to have discouraged foreign imports from the 1960s by creating difficult requirements and customs barriers as a way of protecting its own industries, particularly the automobile industry. And although the growth in world trade may have been affected by Japanese protectionism, who can say that these policies were wrong in the long term? The evidence suggests that they helped make Japan one of the world's leading economies.

Subsidies and inward investment

Another way in which governments may influence firms and businesses is by offering subsidies, less regulation, or lower taxes to businesses in order to encourage them to invest in certain areas, perhaps in poor districts that have particularly high rates of unemployment. An early example of this policy was a lenient law on trusts passed by the state of New Jersey in 1899 to encourage Standard Oil, then involved in the debate over trusts and monopolies, to base itself there.

LEFT: Some people argue that tobacco companies have too much influence in Congress as a result of their large contributions to election funds.

59

The most visible example of this practice in the United States recently has been the efforts of many southern states to encourage Japanese and German car manufacturers to build factories on their land. States such as Alabama, Kentucky, and Tennessee have given firms like Nissan and Saturn relief from corporate taxes, grants to build new roads and drain swampland, and money to train their U.S. workforce. For example, in 1993 Alabama gave a package of subsidies and tax breaks worth a total of $250 million to Mercedes Benz when the German corporation decided to build a new factory in Tuscaloosa County. This was then the largest such payment ever made by a U.S. state to a foreign investor. Some people think it is wrong for states to pay taxpayers' money to foreign firms as a "reward" for inward investment.

In order to minimize the controversy surrounding such projects, U.S. states often announce that taxpayers' money is actually being used to construct buildings and educate workers, rather than being given directly to foreign firms as subsidies. If the foreign firm would otherwise have spent these sums itself anyway, it might be argued that the states are actually paying rewards for investment.

Taxation

Government looks to business for a large proportion of its tax revenues (*see* Taxes, page 79). However, the taxation of business is a subject of debate. Taxes are paid on profits; and so in big corporations, which pay the vast majority of business taxes, they are effectively paid by the companies' shareholders, who have saved their earnings in order to buy shares. Because taxes on profits penalize people for saving, economists generally believe there should be no taxes on business profits but only on individuals' spending. Most governments do tax business profits, however, perhaps because it is relatively easy for them to do so: businesses are often large organizations that cannot hide or run away, and they are legally obliged to keep accurate records.

SEE ALSO:

• Volume 2, page 28: How a business works

• Volume 2, page 100: Market failure and externalities

• Volume 5, page 14: Competition and perfect competition

• Volume 5, page 19: Corporations

• Volume 5, page 38: Externalities and government policy

• Volume 5, page 51: Intellectual property

• Volume 5, page 57: Labor

• Volume 5, page 74: Monopoly

• Volume 5, page 89: Public sector

• Volume 5, page 93: Regulation and antitrust laws

• Volume 5, page 107: Taxation, taxes and subsidies

• Volume 6, page 54: Industrialization, urbanization, and modernization

Government and labor

There are some 6 billion people on the planet, making them one of the most powerful economic resources of all. Not all are available to work: some are too young or too old, others are too ill. Those that remain make up the "workforce."

Labor is the physical and mental human effort involved in the production process. Economists generally differentiate between labor and entrepreneurial activity, where entrepreneurial activity is the management and organization of production processes, coupled with the willingness to take risks. Both of these are human contributions to production, but the role of the entrepreneur is sufficiently important to warrant separate treatment.

Labor is people

Traditional economic theory treats labor as any other productive resource and uses the tools of market analysis to examine decisions in the labor market. The quantity of labor is usually measured in hours, and the price is simply the hourly wage. The labor market is composed of all the buyers and sellers of labor, i.e., firms and corporations, and workers/employees. Despite this, labor clearly is not just like any other resource. Labor is also people—people who may be (and frequently have been) grossly exploited.

This is a central problem with the simple application of economic analysis to labor. It is also one of the reasons governments intervene in labor markets. So, for example, government might regulate conditions of work and might regulate labor unions and business relations with unions; governments also often provide employment exchanges, and most in the developed world will also provide some kind of unemployment compensation.

There are also a number of key economic, as opposed to ethical, differences between labor and other productive resources. Perhaps the most obvious difference is that labor cannot be bought, but only rented. That is, unless you are willing to consider a return to slavery! Another key difference between the way traditional economic theory treats labor and the way labor exists in the economy is that labor is both multidimensional and heterogeneous. This means that there are as many different kinds of labor as there are different kinds of people. Strength, intelligence, training, and interpersonal skills are but a few examples of the ways in which workers can be different. Similarly, there are many kinds of jobs. Traditionally, people are thought of as working full time, but over the last several decades part-time work, job-sharing arrangements, and temporary work have become more commonplace and more important.

ABOVE: *Labor is the physical and mental human effort in the production process. Some less traditional jobs, such as that of this aerial stuntman, require more physical and mental effort than others.*

Major trends in the labor market

U.S. government intervention into labor markets has greatly increased during the 20th century, particularly since the Great Depression of the 1930s and the social welfare legislation that came in as part of the New Deal. A number of broad trends have also emerged that have had an influence on labor and on this role of government.

The past 100 years have seen the U.S. economy roughly doubling in size. This growth was not simply the result of an expansion of existing industries but was caused by a combination of factors. Two of the most important were the decline in manufacturing and the rise in service industries.

The dawn of the 20th century saw western economies in the midst of a period in which mass production technology was being widely implemented. This led to vast increases in the scale of manufacturing operations and output. Throughout the century these manufacturing technologies have become increasingly automated, and the role of employees has changed to reflect this. Fewer employees are now required to produce the same output

in these industries. However, as dramatically as manufacturing employment has fallen, employment in service industries has increased—that is, in medical professions, in legal services, and so forth.

According to data from the U.S. Bureau of Labor Statistics, the total U.S. workforce grew from 27 million people in 1919 to nearly 126 million in 1998. Over this same period the number of workers involved in the production of manufactured goods has risen from 10.6 million to 18.7 million. Those workers involved in the production of goods (some of which are manufactured goods) increased from 12.8 million to 25.3 million workers over the same period. Look at these numbers in more detail. Manufacturing workers made up just under 40 percent of the workforce in 1919. By 1998 they represented just under 15 percent of the workforce. The share of workers involved in goods production fell from 47 percent in 1919 to 20 percent in 1998. The real growth in the workforce occurred in the service sector. Service industry employment grew from 14.3 million workers in 1919 to 100.5 million in 1998. The share of employees involved in service production rose from just under 53 percent in 1919 to nearly 80 percent by 1998.

ABOVE: In 1919 manufacturing workers, such as these men and women at work in a textile factory in California, made up just under 40 percent of the laborforce. By 1998 manufacturing workers represented just under 15 percent.

LEFT: *Lilian Walsh starts her training on a turret lathe in the engine shop of the Philadelphia Navy Yard in March 1942. The acquisition of new skills, receipt of wages, and the resulting feelings of a new independence brought about by the war were to change women's working habits forever.*

Rosie the Riveter

War obviously has an influence on the role of government; it, in turn, can have a major effect on labor market trends. The U.S. entered the war in December 1941. This brought rapid economic and social changes. The military draft reduced the number of men in the workforce, and by the end of 1942 there was a shortage of manpower that was seen to be affecting industrial output. The War Manpower Commission targeted women—many of whom were not part of the workforce—and began a public relations campaign aimed at attracting women to do industrial jobs essential to the war effort–Rosie the Riveter was born.

The success of this campaign is not only seen in the fact that during the following five years over six million women joined the workforce. It also revealed a changing attitude toward working women. During the Depression, rather than try to find work to supplement their family's income, women decided to stay at home and leave the jobs to "Dad." Employed women at the time received more contempt than praise. But between 1942 and 1944 women joined men in steel mills, munitions factories, shipyards, and aircraft factories.

The biggest problem for many women who wanted to work was a lack of childcare provision. Few companies offered any help, with the famous exception of Boeing in Seattle, which offered day care, nursing care, and advise to working mothers.

"Rosie the Riveter," star of the campaign and representative

of the new women workers, was patriotic, home loving, and wanted to help win the war and bring her man home sooner. She was also willing to go back to the way things were when the war ended. Or was she?

At the end of the war women were encouraged to return to their prewar domestic lives, and by 1946 there were four million fewer women working than there had been in 1944. However, a national poll taken in 1945 suggested that three in four women would, given the choice, keep their jobs. Women had been trained, had earned money and respect. As the postwar economy expanded, many women returned to work. By 1950 the number of working women had nearly reached its wartime peak, although they were, by and large, in lower-paid occupations.

Still, it is a remarkable statistic that when the U.S. entered the war following the Japanese attack on Pearl Harbor, women made up 25 percent of the workforce. Five years later that figure had risen to 36 percent, a larger increase than that of the previous 40 years combined.

In the United States the workforce participation rate—the percentage of people of working age who either have jobs or are looking for work—was 58.8 percent in 1948. By 1998 this rate had risen to 67.1 percent. Importantly, women have entered the workforce in increasing numbers since World War II. The traditional family unit with the husband as the sole earner and the wife involved in nonmarket labor (e.g., household chores and childcare) has become less and less common. While the overall workforce participation rate has increased, male participation has actually fallen from 86.6 percent in 1948 to 74.9 percent in 1998. This decline is more than offset by an increase in the participation rate for women. In 1948 only 32.7 percent of working age women were part of the workforce; by 1998 this figure had risen to 59.8 percent.

The above trends, particularly the increased presence of women in the workforce, have had many effects: some economic, and some social. For example, the increase in dual-earner families can be credited with spawning new industries such as childcare services, convenience foods, and domestic services. At the same time, the changing nature of employment implies a role for government—for example, in supporting people who have lost jobs or who cannot find work as old industries close and others become more mechanized, and in retraining and matching people to new jobs.

Wage determination and reasons for wage differentials

The market that allocates workers to jobs and coordinates employment decisions is called the labor market. The labor market is regarded just like any other market discussed in economics. And just like almost any other market, it can be subject to market failure. Government might intervene to correct or reduce the impact of this market failure (*see* page 73). The labor market is composed of buyers (employers) and sellers (employees). To examine the interaction of these groups, it is useful to use the tools of market analysis: demand and supply.

Labor demand

Many factors influence the demand for labor, but one insight can unify these factors. The first thing to note is that the demand for labor is a derived demand. This means that employers do not buy labor because of any inherent utility they receive from employing workers, but instead because labor can be used to produce goods and services that can be sold to generate revenue. Thus the demand for labor is derived from the demand for output. Put simply, the amount employers are willing to pay to hire labor depends on how much revenue that labor will produce.

BELOW: A chocolate firm uses labor to produce goods that can be sold to generate revenue. The amount they are willing to pay for this labor depends on how much revenue the labor will produce.

Formally, this idea is implemented via the Marginal Revenue Product (MRP) of labor. The MRP is simply the value of the output produced by the last unit of labor employed by the firm. The MRP can be broken down further. The MRP is the Marginal Physical Product (MPP) of labor (the number of units of output produced by the last unit of labor) multiplied by the price of output.

For example, a chocolate firm is currently producing 100,000 pounds of hand-wrapped chocolates each day, and the price charged for the chocolate is $0.50 per pound. Now suppose the chocolate firm asks one employee to work an additional hour, and that as a result of this extra hour of labor the firm produces 20 extra pounds of chocolate that day. Total revenue for the firm rises from $50,000 (100,000 pounds x $0.50/pound) to $50,010 (100,020 pounds x $0.50/pound) for the day. In this case the MRP is $10. It can also be calculated by multiplying the amount of additional output (the Marginal Physical Product: in this case 20 pounds) by the price level.

Table 1 (right) presents another example that helps clarify the concepts of MPP and MRP. It can be seen that MRP declines as the number of people employed increases. This is due to the law of diminishing returns. Holding all other factors of production constant (such as land and capital), output can be increased by increasing the amount of labor employed, but only at a decreasing rate. At low levels of employment it is possible to add additional employees, additional shifts, etc. An increasing MRP might be expected at very low levels of employment due to gains from specialization. At higher levels of employment, however, there are simply more employees than can make effective use of the other inputs. For

Labor hours	Total output	MPP	Output price	Revenue	MRP
0	0	–	10	0	–
1	10	10	10	100	100
2	19	9	10	190	90
3	27	8	10	270	80
4	34	7	10	340	70
5	40	6	10	400	60
6	45	5	10	450	50
7	49	4	10	490	40
6	52	3	10	520	30
7	54	2	10	540	20
8	55	1	10	550	10
9	55	0	10	550	0
10	54	-1	10	540	-10

Table 1 Number of labor hours demanded will be where the wage equals MRP.

ABOVE & LEFT: A general understanding of how much people want to work is aided by considering that the decision about how much time to devote to work is intimately linked to the concept of leisure time. If you don't work, you won't have the money to play soccer, go skateboarding, or have a good time in Las Vegas.

example, maintenance schedules may be compromised as extra time in production substitutes for this "down time." At very high levels of employment the MRP becomes negative as additional employees get in each other's way.

In conclusion, labor demand is determined by the value of the output labor produces. Firms will demand sufficient labor to make the wage paid equal to the MRP. This is because if the wage is lower than the MRP, then it would be possible for the firm to hire additional labor and make additional profit. For example, if the wage was $10.00/hour and the MRP was $12.00, then the firm could spend $10.00 for another hour of labor and generate $12.00 in extra revenue. The firm could generate an extra $2.00 in profit. Similarly, if the wage is more than the MRP, a firm can raise profits by cutting back on the labor it employs. Thus firms will demand a quantity of labor such that the wage equals the MRP.

Labor supply

What determines how much people want to work? Each person undoubtedly has different reasons for his or her specific choice, but our general understanding is aided by thinking of the quantity of labor supplied in conjunction with another good: leisure time. The decision about how much time to devote to work is intimately linked to the concept of leisure time.

Note that there is a finite amount of time available to each individual. There are only 24 hours in a day. Now suppose there are only two ways to spend the time available: labor

and leisure. Labor is time spent working. Leisure is time spent doing anything other than working. This is, of course, a simplification, but it is essentially true.

Thinking of both labor and leisure together helps us understand the nature of the labor supply decision. If you spend all of your time working, then you have no time available to sleep, eat, read, watch television, or do anything other than work. If you devote all your time to leisure pursuits, unless you have a private income, your options are severely limited. You have no income with which to purchase the goods and services that make leisure time worth having. Unless you work, you would have no money for food, housing, televisions, books, plane tickets, cars, etc. It is not surprising that most people choose to work several hours each week.

Equilibrium in the labor market

The labor market is said to be in equilibrium when the quantity of labor demanded by employers precisely equals the quantity of labor supplied by workers. This equilibrium is represented by the intersection of the labor demand and labor supply curves (see Figure 1). Opposing forces mean that the labor market tends to move toward this equilibrium point. Let's consider each of two possibilities in turn. First, that the market wage is below the level consistent with the proposed equilibrium; and second, that it is above this level.

Suppose that the market wage is below the proposed equilibrium value. At this level the quantity of labor demanded is greater than the quantity of labor supplied. Put differently,

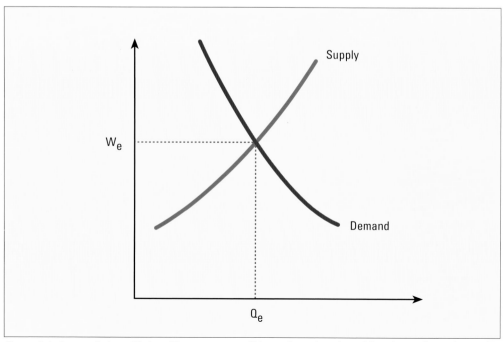

Figure 1 Labor market equilibrium. The wage rate will be at the point where labor demand equals supply.

there is a shortage of labor. Some employers would like to employ more workers than they can attract at the current wage level. What should these firms do? The obvious way to attract additional workers is to increase the wage level. Firms' profits will increase with such wage increases so long as the amount they are paying the additional workers remains below the MRP of these workers. As the market wage rises, we observe an increase in the quantity of labor supplied and a decrease in the quantity of labor demanded. This is represented as movement along the labor supply and labor demand curves. Thus, for wage levels below our proposed equilibrium level there is a tendency for wages to rise.

It is also important to determine what happens at wage levels above the proposed equilibrium value in order to accept the proposed equilibrium. At such wage levels the quantity of labor demanded is less than the quantity of labor supplied. There is a surplus of labor. There are people willing and able to work at the going wage rate who can not find work. This is unemployment. Some of these unemployed workers would be willing to work for a wage below the current wage, and they will bid down the market wage in an attempt to find work. As the market wage falls in response to this process, it is possible to observe an increase in the quantity of labor demanded and a decrease in the quantity of labor supplied. This is represented by movement along the labor demand and labor supply curves. Thus, for wage levels above the proposed equilibrium level there is a tendency for wages to fall. However, it may be that wages will not automatically adjust, moving

demand and supply back to equilibrium levels. This might be as a result of union pressures or minimum wage legislation passed by government (see page 70 and page 77).

Determinants of labor demand and labor supply

Labor demand and labor supply are not constants. There are many things that influence how much labor people choose to supply to the market and how much labor firms want to purchase.

Determinants of demand for labor

The marginal revenue product of labor lies at the core of labor demand, and anything that alters the MRP will shift the labor demand relationship. First, suppose that the demand for the output of a particular industry increases. As a result, more of the output could be sold than before at any given output price, and therefore the equilibrium output price would rise. Remember that the MRP is simply the MPP multiplied by output price. The increase in the equilibrium output price shifts the MRP to the right and so represents an increase in labor demand. In practical terms this means that if demand for output such as lobsters goes up, more fishermen will be required to supply them.

Similarly, the effects of change in the price of another input to the production process can be analyzed. Suppose the cost of capital falls by 50 percent. In other words, suppose that the cost of obtaining plant and equipment fell so much that firms could purchase twice

BELOW: Some industries are more labor intensive than others. This pineapple packing plant in Honolulu, for example, requires a large labor force to do work that cannot be mechanized.

as much plant and equipment as before for precisely the same amount of money. The fall in capital costs will cause the supply of output to increase, and the equilibrium price of output will fall. Again, remember that the MRP is simply the MPP multiplied by output price. Thus the fall in capital costs shifts the MRP to the left: this represents a decrease in labor demand. In practical terms this means that if the price of car-making robots goes down, then the demand for (now relatively expensive) car workers will fall as manufacturers turn to capital-intensive techniques.

Both of these examples have taken the MPP as given. Now suppose that something happens to affect the fundamental productivity of the workforce (e.g., new skills training or better education of the workforce). An increase in labor productivity (i.e., the MPP) increases the MRP and generates an increase in labor demand. Ultimately, anything other than the market wage and the quantity of labor that affects the MPP or output price will shift the labor demand curve.

Determinants of supply of labor
The quantity of labor supplied to the market depends on a wide variety of things. The motivation to work, income taxes, unemployment compensation, population growth, and the workforce participation rate can all influence labor supply. Anything that increases

work effort, the number of workers in a particular market, or the workforce participation rate will increase labor supply. Conversely, anything decreasing these items will decrease labor supply.

The motivation to work is affected by many things, and one of the most often discussed determinants of this motivation is income tax. Suppose the income tax rate was 100 percent. This would mean that any income earned through the labor market would be paid to the government in taxes. It

ABOVE: Some high tech industries are highly mechanized and controlled by computers. The output of industries such as this compressor assembly company is achieved with little labor but with a massive outlay on machinery.

LEFT: The output of certain industries, such as this computer assembly plant, are relatively labor-intensive and make quite limited use of capital inputs.

is not difficult to see why there would be little motivation to work if the income tax rate was 100 percent. This extreme example illustrates the relationship between income tax rates—which are set by government—and labor supply. The debate is about just how large this effect is in the economy, and what effect any given change in tax rates will have on labor supply.

Population growth is obviously important. When new workers reach working age, they will begin looking for work. Less obvious is the effect of the workforce participation rate. As discussed earlier, the workforce participation rate is the ratio of the workforce to the total number of people of working age. If the workforce participation rate increases (holding the population constant), the size of the workforce must be rising, and this will increase labor supply.

In summary, the shape of the labor supply curve depends on the tradeoff between work and leisure, and is upward sloping. This curve shifts when there are changes in work effort, in the workforce participation rate, and in population. All else being equal, any increase in labor supply will increase the amount of labor employed in the market and decrease the market wage. As mentioned before, however, a simple adjustment of the wage rate to reflect changes in demand or supply will not always occur in labor markets.

Relaxing assumptions

Many simplifying assumptions are built into the equilibrium in the labor market developed above. Chief among them is the idea that

there is some homogeneous asset called labor that sells at an hourly rate. Even a cursory examination of the economy reveals that this is not the case.

There is wide variety in the way employees are paid. In addition to the hourly wage discussed above, many workers are paid a salary—that is, a fixed amount regardless of the number of hours they work. This type of arrangement is more common among management or professional workers than among production workers. Fringe benefits, such as health insurance and firm-subsidized pension plans, are another important part of the pay package of many employees.

Many employees receive some portion of their pay through mechanisms like profit-shar-

ABOVE & BELOW: One of the puzzles facing economists is the existence of unjustifiable wage differentials commonly based on racial and gender differences. However, in higher paid occupations these differentials are less evident.

69

ing, bonuses, and other forms of incentive plans. Douglas Kruse reports in *Profit Sharing: Does It Make a Difference?* (1993) that depending on which data series is examined, between one-sixth and one-quarter of United States employees and firms participate in profit-sharing. Profit-sharing is not new. The percentage of firms using profit-sharing systems has remained between 19 and 23 percent since 1963. Kruse finds that on average, the adoption of profit-sharing systems leads to productivity increases of between 3.5 and 5 percent. These increases appear to be higher for small firms than for large firms. While the average increases are positive, there is considerable variation in the results of individual firms, so profit-sharing systems are by no means guaranteed to be successful.

Kruse also finds some evidence that employment levels in profit-sharing firms are more stable than employment levels in other firms. This may be because the design of firms with profit-sharing systems leads to automatic decreases in pay during periods of low demand, and this may reduce the pressure on firms to layoff workers.

Last, there does not seem to be anything as simple as a market wage. One of the puzzles facing economists who analyze data from labor markets is the presence of unjustifiable wage differentials. Some workers will have different skills, education levels, experience,

etc., and these attributes will all influence the wage any individual employee will receive. However, even when these differences between workers are recognized, there are significant differences in levels of pay among workers. The two most common are gender and racial differences. The average white, female, full-time worker can expect to earn roughly 68 percent of what the average white, male, full-time worker earns. This discrepancy is only partly accounted for by occupation and other factors. There is still a 10-15 percent gap in wages between otherwise identical men and women. A similar gap sometimes exists between people of different ethnic origins.

This implies a role for government in terms of legislation to address such discrepancies. It also implies a role for employee organization in the form of labor unions.

The role of labor unions

The efforts of labor unions have led to significant changes in the nature of the employer-employee relationship in the modern economy.

Though national organization of U.S. employees began in the middle of the 19th century, the modern labor movement traces its roots to the founding of the American Federation of Labor (AFL) in 1881. The AFL

ABOVE: Members of the Carpenters Union at a strike rally in New York City in 1997. At the beginning of the 21st century many of the traditional causes that the unions stood up for have been enshrined by law. Nontraditional issues, such as race and gender, seem likely to be at the top of the unions' agendas for the new millennium.

was a federation of craft unions. A craft union represents members with specific work skills, and the AFL membership was composed of unions representing electricians, carpenters, printers, etc.

This craft union structure proved ill-suited to the industrial age because with the rise of the factory system, labor organizers found they had more influence if they could speak for all of the workers in a factory with one voice, rather than representing several competing crafts. This gave rise to industrial unions, composed of all the workers in an industry, regardless of their craft. The Congress of Industrial Organizations (CIO), formed in 1935, was an industrial union. The present day United Auto Workers union (UAW) is an excellent example of an industrial union. Anyone working in an automobile plant in the United States qualifies for membership in the UAW. The AFL and CIO merged in 1955 to form the AFL/CIO. The AFL/CIO was one of the most significant political forces in the United States in the 20th century.

Labor unions are organizations designed to create and exercise power in the labor market. A labor union attempts to be the sole seller of labor in a given market. Economists refer to this single-seller environment as a monopsony. Were a group of firms to collude in an attempt to keep wages low, they would be

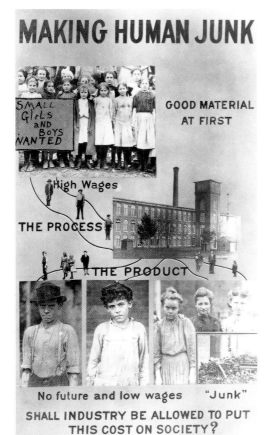

The National Labor Relations Board (NLRB)

The NLRB is an independent federal agency with two main functions. First, it oversees secret-ballot elections through which employees may decide whether they wish to be represented by a union when dealing with their employers. Second, it ensures that employers and unions do not engage in unfair labor practices.

Employers may not:
- Threaten employees with loss of jobs or benefits if they join or vote for a union or engage in protected concerted activity.
- Threaten to close the plant if employees select a union to represent them.
- Question employees about their union sympathies or activities in circumstances that tend to interfere with, restrain, or coerce employees in the exercise of their rights under the National Labor Relations Act.
- Promise benefits to employees to discourage their union support.
- Transfer, lay off, terminate, or assign employees more difficult work tasks because they are engaged in union or protected concerted activity.

Unions may not:
- Threaten employees that they will lose their jobs unless they support the union's activities.
- Refuse to process a grievance because an employee has criticized union officers.
- Fine employees who have validly resigned from the union for engaging in protected activity following their resignation.
- Seek the discharge of an employee for not complying with a union shop agreement when the employee has paid or offered to pay a lawful initiation fee and periodic dues.
- Refuse referral or give preference in a hiring hall on the basis of race or union activities.

The NLRB does not seek out unfair labor practices. It only processes those charges filed by employers or unions. When an unfair labor practice charge is filed, NLRB investigates whether there is reasonable cause to believe a violation has occurred. If this investigation finds reasonable cause to believe a violation has been committed, the NLRB seeks a voluntary settlement. If settlement efforts fail, a formal complaint is issued, and the case goes to hearing before an NLRB Administrative Law Judge. The judge issues a written decision that may be appealed to the NLRB, and this decision is subject to review in a U.S. Court of Appeals.

Depending on the nature of the case, the goal is to complete investigations and issue complaints if settlement is not reached within 7 to 15 weeks from the filing of the charge. Of the total charges filed each year (about 35,000) approximately one-third are found to have merit, of which over 90 percent are settled out of court.

LEFT: This union poster, published in 1910, is representative of an anti-child labor campaign. This issue was central to the union movement in the early years of the 20th century and is now enshrined by law in most western countries.

LEFT: *Potato picking in Idaho. Although highly mechanized, farmers still need a substantial increase in the number of laborers they employ during the potato harvest.*

Year	All civilian workers	Males	Females	Both sexes 16-19 years	White	Black and other
1951	3.3	2.8	4.4	8.2	3.1	5.3
1955	4.4	4.2	4.9	11.0	3.9	8.7
1959	5.5	5.2	5.9	14.6	4.8	10.7
1963	5.7	5.2	6.5	17.2	5.0	10.8
1967	3.8	3.1	5.2	12.9	3.4	7.4
1971	5.9	5.3	6.9	16.9	5.4	9.9
1975	8.5	7.9	9.3	19.9	7.8	13.8
1979	5.8	5.1	6.8	16.1	5.1	11.3
1983	9.6	9.9	9.2	22.4	8.4	17.8
1987	6.2	6.2	6.2	16.9	5.3	11.6
1991	6.7	7.0	6.3	18.9	6.0	11.1
1995	5.6	5.6	5.6	17.3	4.9	9.6
1997	5.0	4.2	4.4	16.0	4.2	8.8

1 Unemployed as a percentage of the civilian labor force in the group specified.

Source: *Economic Report of the President, 1995 (Washington, D.C.: U.S. Government Printing Office, 1998), page 320.*

Table 2 The unemployment rate for civilian workers in the United States, 1951-1997[1].

considered to be forming a monopoly, and thus be in violation of the Sherman Antitrust Act (1890). However, groups of employees are allowed to collude via unions to keep wages high because The Clayton Act of 1914 removed organized labor from antitrust prosecution. This was because the government of the time felt that certain loopholes had been left in the Sherman Act, and large corporations still held a disproportionate degree of power. The Clayton Act sought to redress this balance of power to some degree in favor of the perceived underdogs, the workers.

The U.S. government's attitude to organized labor is demonstrated by the associated legislation passed by Congress. The Clayton Act made the modern labor movement possible in the first place, for example. Later pieces of legislation also affected unions and labor relations to a significant degree. The Railway Labor Act (1926) established the legality of collective bargaining. The Norris-La Guardia Act (1932) limited the power of the federal government to become involved in labor disputes. The Wagner Act (1935) gave all employees the right to organize and also established the National Labor Relations Board (*see* box, page 71). The Taft-Hartley Act (1947), however, sought to swing the balance of power back toward employers by allowing the government to impose an 80-day "cooling off" period to stop strikes. Taft-Hartley grants this power only for strikes that endanger public health or safety. In addition, Taft-Hartley outlawed the closed shop.

Labor unions today face an interesting dilemma. Many of the rights unions fought for in the early stages of the labor movement have been enshrined in the legal and regulatory systems of most western economies. Laws against child labor, increased safety regulation, overtime pay, disability payments, minimum wages, etc., have all been accepted into the fabric of the labor market in the United States, Europe, Australia, and elsewhere. Given that this is the case, what is the role of labor unions today?

Union membership in the United States has been falling steadily for the last 30 years, and recent efforts to combat this have focused on recruiting minority workers and women. They are groups that have traditionally avoided labor union membership, but racial and gender equality are obvious issues to carry labor unions into the 21st century.

Labor market failure

In the idealized world of economic theory labor markets are simple. These markets behave just like any other: quantity supplied and quantity demanded adjust to capture all

possible gains in profit and utility. In this equilibrium real wages equal the marginal productivity of labor, and there is no surplus or shortage of labor at this price. There is no unemployment. The greatest good for the greatest number is obtained by simply allowing the market mechanism to set wages and allocate labor.

But in the real world matters are not so simple. Economics uses the term "market failure" to describe any situation where the price mechanism does not result in the best possible outcome in a market. The following subsections examine certain types of labor market failures that result in different kinds of unemployment.

Unemployment
Economics says unemployment exists in an economy if labor supply exceeds labor demand at the prevailing wage rate. Put simply, there are more people offering to work than there are jobs available. More for-

ABOVE: *During the 1980s the U.S. steel industry was subjected to intense foreign competition, which meant that the number of people employed in the U.S. fell dramatically.*

mally, unemployment is the fraction of those people willing and able to work at the going wage who cannot find work at this wage rate. See Table 2, page 72, on unemployment statistics for additional detail. There are several kinds of unemployment: seasonal, cyclical, structural, and frictional.

Seasonal unemployment

Unemployment caused by seasonal fluctuations in labor supply and labor demand is called seasonal unemployment. Apple pickers. Christmas retail staff. Beach lifeguards. These are just three examples of types of jobs that are affected by such seasonal factors. There are some jobs that only exist at certain times of year. Orchardists need relatively few employees except during the brief harvest season. The ripening of the apple crop creates a large temporary increase in labor demand. Those people who are without work because demand for their skills is "out of season" are said to be seasonally unemployed.

Cyclical unemployment

Cyclical unemployment reflects the decline in total output that occurs in recessionary phases of the business cycle. Cyclical unemployment is similar in character to seasonal unemployment, but the length of the "season" is not so obvious or reliable.

There are strong cyclical patterns in the performance of market economies. During boom times (i.e., when real GDP growth is high), firms raise wages in an attempt to obtain the workers they need to maximize profits. In bust times (when real GDP growth

is negative) wages (or at least real wages) fall because firms no longer need so much labor, and firms may lay off workers they do not need under current economic conditions. Those people who are without work because there is a temporary lack of demand for their skills are said to be cyclically unemployed.

Structural unemployment

Structural unemployment is generated when changes in tastes, technology, taxes, or competition from foreign countries reduce the demand for certain skills. Those workers whose skills are simply no longer in demand are said to be structurally unemployed.

The case of U.S. steelworkers is a good example. Through the 1980s the U.S. steel industry underwent major structural changes and was subjected to intense foreign competition, which meant that the number of steelworkers required in the United States fell dramatically.

This shift was mirrored in other industries as part of the general shift of the U.S. economy from a manufacturing base to a service industry base (see page 62). There were many employees whose skills in their previous jobs were simply no longer needed in the current marketplace. Structural unemployment is particularly worrying because it is not something that self-corrects quickly like seasonal fluctuations or cyclical fluctuations. It takes time for employees to retrain. It also takes money to acquire new skills, and of course such expenditures are particularly problematic for the unemployed, although the government may intervene with retraining programs.

Frictional unemployment

Frictional unemployment refers to the level of unemployment that results from the healthy functioning of a market economy. For example, there will always be people who quit jobs to look for better ones. An example helps clarify this point. Suppose a woman working in New York is offered a significant promotion, but the new job is in Los Angeles. The woman's move to the new job does not create any impact on unemployment figures directly because she is moving straight from one job to another. However, if the woman has a family, this may change things. Suppose the move to Los Angeles means that her husband must give up his current job and seek a new one in Los Angeles. While the husband looks for new work, he will be registered as unemployed in the statistics.

At any point in time nearly half of all those people looking for work have either quit their last job, are reentering the workforce, or are new entrants to the workforce. Most of these people can be counted as frictionally unemployed. Frictional unemployment is simply an outgrowth of the reallocation of labor to its most valued use. Frictional unemployment seldom lasts for long and usually results in a better match of employees to jobs. This is why we refer to frictional unemployment as a welcome part of a healthy economy.

Underemployment

People are said to be underemployed if they are currently in work but are working in a job that does not maximize their marginal productivity. The Great Depression contains many examples of this problem. One interesting literary treatment of the plight of ordinary people during this time is *The Wonder Book of the Air*, by Cynthia Shearer (1996). One of the characters in this book is Uncle Artie, a man with a physics degree from Georgia Tech who worked as a radio engineer in St. Louis before the Depression. The economic collapse caused him to lose his job, and he moved home to live with his extended family in Georgia. He became the local radio repairman to pay his way. There were so many other things a man with his education could have done, but fixing radios was the only thing available. The book provides a stark picture of life in Depression era America; and while Uncle Artie is a fictional character, he serves as an excellent example of underemployment.

Full employment

Full employment is said to exist when cyclical unemployment is zero. Full employment does not mean that there is no unemployment. There will still be unemployed people due to seasonal, structural, and frictional effects.

A fair pay for a fair day's work?

Over the past 150 years many people have argued that workers do not see the full rewards of their toil, and that this is one of the central injustices of capitalism. It was Marx who first put forward the idea that capitalist production is essentially an exploitative system whereby capitalists, the owners of factories and businesses, reap the rewards of production, leaving the people who actually do the work as beggars at the feast.

Central to this argument is the concept of surplus value. Production involves combining factors such as land, natural resources, raw materials, capital goods–factory buildings, machinery, and tools–and labor to produce finished goods. Labor is treated just as if it were any other input into the production process. The finished goods produced in this way actually have a higher value than the cost of the factors that have gone into them in the first place–this is known as surplus value. Marx's point was that a worker could "produce his salary" in, for example, 6 or 7 hours, but would actually work more hours than this each day (the working day was around 12 to 15 hours at the time Marx was writing). During these extra hours the worker produces a "surplus" product–goods for which he or she receives no extra pay.

This surplus product gives surplus value and represents extra profit for the capitalists. Under this system increasing worker productivity –improving training and skills so that he or she produces more output–increases surplus value. Hence a rise in worker productivity will increase the extra profit made by capitalists but will not benefit workers in any way. Workers are, in fact, relatively worse off–their wages are worse in relation to the profits made by the capitalists. Marx contended that this would lead to competition between capitalists and workers as capitalists try to increase their profits and workers try to resist, a struggle that would eventually lead to the downfall of capitalism.

Despite the unionization of labor and modern-day improvements in salaries, working conditions, and the number of hours people work, at least in industrialized countries, some would argue that Marx's theory of surplus value still has relevance for many workers today.

Since 1950 the full employment rate has risen from around 4 percent to 5-6 percent.

The full employment rate is worthy of close attention by policy makers. Demand management policies are appropriate tools for addressing cyclical unemployment but would be poorly suited to addressing, for example, structural unemployment. Retraining programs would be far better suited for this particular problem.

Labor market failure: the role of government

When markets yield efficient and equitable results, there is little role for government intervention. However, in the real world markets do not always yield efficient and equitable results. Unemployment, vastly unequal income distributions, minimal safety provisions, discriminatory practices, and many other undesirable effects may (and often do) result from the market mechanism. In these cases the government may wish to intervene in an attempt to correct, or at least improve, the situation.

Governments in the developed world attempt to correct labor market failures through, for example, paying unemployment compensation to those in the workforce who

are unable to find work and disability payments for those who are unable to work for health reasons. Such payments enable people to survive while they are looking for work, while they are retraining, or if they are unable to work for an extended period.

Most Western nations also have child labor restrictions, equal opportunity legislation, comparable worth legislation, and occupational safety codes to prevent exploitation of workers by unscrupulous employers (see Government and the individual, page 28).

ABOVE: The evidence as to whether a minimum wage is good for the economy cuts both ways. Traditional economic theory says it increases unemployment, while more modern research links minimum wages with increased employment.

Figure 2 The value of the minimum wage in the United States, 1938-1997.

Legislation is normally enforced through various government agencies and boards (*see* Organizations and boards, page 105). Many governments also impose a minimum wage, a wage below which it is deemed to be exploitative of employers to ask people to work. Minimum wage legislation is a particularly contentious form of government intervention into labor markets (*see* below).

Each of these programs is designed to solve a particular problem in the market, but many create their own difficulties. Governments must trade off the benefits of such programs against the costs: the financial and social costs, and the costs in terms of incentives and output-foregone.

Policy tradeoffs

The presumption is that governments should only intervene in markets if they can improve the situation. There is much debate about just how equitable and efficient labor markets are, and consequently what role may exist for government in setting policy.

When governments do set policies, they must consider the costs and benefits of their actions, as mentioned above. This is not an easy process. The costs of unemployment, for example, include loss of output and income. This in turn has an effect on the economy as a whole, reducing aggregate demand and supply as people have less disposable income to spend on goods and services. There are also costs in terms of loss of skills and training in the workforce (loss of human capital), rising crime, and the loss of self-esteem and human dignity that is suffered by people who are out of work for a long time.

The benefits of unemployment, on the other hand, are seen by economists in terms of a nation having a flexible workforce where there is room for expansion and change in different sectors, and where people can be better matched to the jobs available. Neither the costs nor the benefits of unemployment are easily measured, however.

Similarly, even something as conceptually simple as setting a minimum wage can create a wide range of interrelated effects. Measuring the costs and benefits of these effects is difficult and the subject of wide debate.

Minimum wage

A minimum wage is the hourly wage below which it is illegal to buy and sell labor. Most Western countries have some form of minimum wage and minimum wage legislation. In the United States the minimum wage was established in 1938 at $0.25/hour, and has been increased occasionally ever since. It was raised to $5.15/hour on September 1,

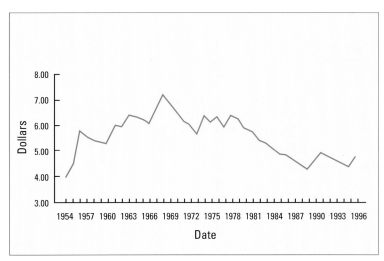

Figure 3 The minimum wage 1954-1996 after adjustments for inflation.

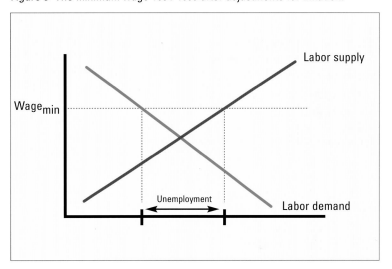

Figure 4 Effects of the minimum wage on employment.

1997. Figure 2 (page 76) shows the adjustments to the minimum wage between 1938 and 1997. Although it has never been lowered, there have been significant periods during which the minimum wage has remained unchanged in the United States. For example, it rose to $3.80 on January 1, 1981, and did not increase again until April 1, 1991, when it was raised to $4.25.

Inflation in the United States during this period eroded the purchasing power of the dollar. Figure 3 (above) shows the purchasing power of the minimum wage through time. You can see that the value of the minimum wage in terms of actual goods and services that could be bought peaked in 1968.

Although the minimum wage has been in place in the United States, and other countries, for many years, the effects of minimum wages on the economy are still hotly debated. Traditional economic theory uses the tools of labor supply and labor demand to demonstrate that a minimum wage set above the prevailing market wage will decrease the overall level of employment as well as generate unemployment. Figure 4 on page 77 demonstrates this prediction. According to this theory, the minimum wage (Wage$_{min}$) results in wages being held artificially high rather than being allowed to fall to a point where the market would be in equilibrium. As a result labor supply exceeds labor demand causing unemployment.

This diagram has been used by many policymakers to argue that minimum wages are bad for the economy, but the issue is not as clear cut as they suggest. If we move away from perfect competition, and away from the idea of labor as a homogeneous commodity, we may find different results.

The evidence cuts both ways. Early studies found that minimum wages actually increased employment. However, this was because such studies failed to account for increases in output demand that more than compensated for the effects of minimum wages. More recent work is divided. Card and Krueger have published a series of papers linking minimum wages with increased employment. Conversely, Neumark and Wascher (1992) and Deere, Murphy, and Welch (1995) find results consistent with traditional economic theory. The minimum wage should continue to be a hot research topic for the foreseeable future.

The poverty trap

Income support for the unemployed is a central feature of modern western economies. As is often the case, the solution to one problem creates another set of problems. The poverty trap refers to the disincentive to work created by such income-support policies.

If an unemployed worker is confronted with the choice between remaining on income support and taking a part-time job in a fast food restaurant, the size of the support payments will figure strongly in the decision to take or reject the job. Unless the job pays more than the income-support program, there is no reason for that individual to take the job. Even a full-time job will have to make quite a difference in some people's incomes for them to consider it worth their while to take the job.

The poverty trap can be a large problem for parents, particularly single parents who are claiming benefits. In this case taking a job not only involves giving up welfare benefits, but also involves giving up child support and making payments out of their wages for childcare. Often the combined effect can add up to considerably more than the compensation offered by many available jobs.

Some of these programs try to soften this disincentive to work by reducing benefits by some fraction of the additional income, but they are difficult to work in practice, and they do not eliminate the disincentive.

SEE ALSO:

• Volume 2, page 6: An introduction to business

• Volume 4, page 6: The U.S. government and world economics

• Volume 5, page 34: Equality and equity

• Volume 5, page 57: Labor

• Volume 5, page 64: Market failure

• Volume 5, page 80: Population

• Volume 5, page 113: Unemployment

• Volume 6, page 54: Industrialization, urbanization, and modernization

LEFT: Single parents with young children often have little choice but to take part-time work. In many cases, however, part-time jobs will not pay much more than the welfare payments they already receive.

Taxes

Every state on earth raises revenues through taxation. Although almost everyone accepts the need for taxes, there has always been deep disagreement about what should be taxed and the exact rate of taxation.

No government can govern effectively without money—to pay its soldiers, policemen, and teachers; to buy land or to fund its bureaucracy; to pay for pensions, healthcare, or building roads. Any government needs a constant supply of revenue. It can come from numerous sources. Governments may raise revenue by printing money, selling natural resources such as land or minerals, or by selling licenses such as taxi-cab medallions or broadcasting rights on radio or TV. The Saudi Arabian government, for example, raises most of its revenue from selling oil.

Raising revenue for the state

By far the most common way for governments to raise revenue, however, is by imposing taxes on their citizens. Taxes are fees imposed by governments on a variety of goods, transactions, and sources of money. Direct taxes, for example, are usually collected from property owners or workers. They include income tax, in which the government takes a certain percentage of every worker's earnings, corporate tax, which takes a share of the profits of all for-profit businesses, and taxes on housing. Inheritance taxes, which people have to pay on any property or money they might inherit, are another form of direct taxation.

Indirect taxation

Indirect taxes are collected from vendors or merchants, or are imposed on specific goods or services. They include highway taxes, in which drivers pay a license fee in order to drive their car on the public highway; sales taxes, in which governments or states take a

ABOVE: Taxation is a complex matter, both in principle and in practice. When filing their tax returns, people must account for all their earnings and understand the regulations—what they have to declare and what they need not.

Taxes in the U.S.

In 1998 the U.S. Federal government had revenues of $ 1.721 trillion.
The vast majority of them came from taxes, as shown in this table.

Source	Amount ($ millions)	Percentage
Individual Income Tax	828,856	48.1
Corporate Income Tax	188,677	11.0
Social Insurance Taxes	571,831	33.2
Other Taxes	100,046	5.8
Other Revenues	32,658	1.9
TOTAL	1,721,798	100.0

Source: Economic Report of the President, 1999, Table B-81.

In this table Other Taxes refers to estate, customs, and excise taxes, such as
the gasoline tax and the tax on the property or estates of the deceased. Other
Revenues are largely the interest earned by the reserves held by the Federal
Reserve, the central bank of the United States. As the table shows, personal
and corporate income taxes now dominate Federal revenues. However, Social
Insurance taxes, the payroll taxes paid specifically to finance Social Security
and Medicare, make up a surprisingly large share of total revenues.

State and local governments also levy a variety of taxes, which collected
around another trillion dollars in 1998. These $2.7 trillion of taxes represented
32.4 percent of U.S. GDP. (In the table opposite, the figure was 32.3 % in
1996.) This percentage is fairly low compared with that of many other
industrialized countries.

RIGHT: Indirect taxes are
levied on spending rather
than on earnings. One of
the main forms of indirect
taxation in the United
States is the sales tax
on every purchase made
in stores.

certain amount of any sales transaction; and
taxes on imported goods. Some economists
argue that there is little distinction between
direct and indirect taxes. They claim that a
direct tax on wages is equivalent to an indirect tax on consumption: no matter from
whom they are collected, the burden of paying taxes eventually falls on the same people,
because all wages eventually go to support
consumption. This is not to say that the
method of taxation makes no difference,
however: different taxes might affect individuals in a variety of different ways.

Progressive and regressive taxation

The impact of a tax will depend largely on
whether it is a progressive, regressive, or proportional tax. A progressive tax is defined as
one that takes a higher percentage of the
incomes of richer people. Progressive taxes
rise or fall in relation to the value of the
income or goods to which they apply: someone who earns $200,000 a year will pay a
higher rate of tax than someone who earns
$50,000. A proportional tax takes the same
proportion of all people's incomes. A tax of 10
percent on everyone's income would be a proportional tax. A regressive tax takes a higher
percentage of poor people's incomes than of
rich people's. A flat-rate tax applied to everyone of say $500 per year regardless of income,

would be regressive. $500 dollars represents a
far greater cost to someone earning $20,000
than it does to someone on $200,000 a year.

Some countries have value-added tax
(VAT), a higher-rate tax imposed on goods
that might be classified as luxuries rather than
necessities, such as basic foodstuffs. What
goods classify as luxuries and are subject to
the tax is often a highly controversial question.
Are books, for example, necessities, or are
they luxuries? If they were liable to VAT,
would that discourage people from reading?

Taxation is one of the most fundamental
ways in which governments influence the
daily lives of their citizens, and it is often
highly controversial. Most people now recognize the necessity of taxation, but some still
protest that governments and other authorities
have no right to claim what they argue is private property. Whatever their viewpoint, virtually everyone has his or her own strong
opinions about how high or low taxes should

Taxes around the world

Taxation in Nine Industrialized Countries in 1996

Country	Taxes as percentage of GDP	Top marginal rate on personal income tax (%)
Canada	44.1	54.1
France	48.6	54.0
Germany	45.0	55.9
Italy	45.6	46.0
Japan	31.7	65.0
South Korea	26.4	44.5
Sweden	61.5	59.6
United Kingdom	38.1	40.0
United States	32.3	39.6

Source: OECD in Figures, OECD, Paris 1999.

European countries such as Sweden, France, and Italy, which have large welfare states, raise much more tax as a proportion of GDP than does the United States. Of the countries listed, only Japan and South Korea levy lighter taxes, although Japan has the highest rate of tax on high earners. Marginal taxes are those paid on an additional dollar or other unit of income. The United States has the lowest top rate of personal income tax in these nine countries.

be, whom they should target, and what the revenue they raise should be used for.

Governments usually set tax rates once or twice a year as part of their budget when they calculate their planned expenditures and the amount of income they need to pay for them. The budget announcement will thus have a direct effect on every citizen in the country. As soon as the tax rates are released, observers and accountants calculate their effect on different people—married or unmarried, high- or low-earning, driver or nondriver—taking into account such variable factors as whether they have children, whether they smoke or drink, the value of their house, and so on.

BELOW: This U.S. sign seems to suggest that less litter would mean less work for cleaners and therefore that fewer tax dollars would be needed to pay for their services.

Political taxation

Taxes are controversial because, as well as using them for the administration of the country, governments can also use them to achieve their political ends. By raising tax on leaded gasoline, for example, some governments hope to encourage drivers to switch to unleaded fuel, thus helping reduce exhaust emissions and pollution. This can work in a government's favor: taxes are traditionally high on goods such as cigarettes and alcohol partly because governments can expect to avoid heavy criticism for taxing such "vices," especially since they can argue that by making such goods more expensive, they are encouraging people to adopt a healthy lifestyle. Other taxes bring governments far more criticism, however. Many people object to paying taxes to fund military armaments, for example, especially if they perceive them as liable to be used in an unpopular conflict rather than in terms of national defense. A striking example of the controversy caused by an unpopular tax came in Britain in the late 1980s.

Britain's poll tax

In 1989 the Conservative government of Margaret Thatcher introduced a so-called poll tax in Scotland and in the rest of Britain the following year. A poll tax is an equal tax on all citizens of voting age, or in some cases on all people who are actually registered to vote. Historically, poll taxes have sometimes been applied in order to exclude people from the right to vote. After the U.S. Civil War, for example, some Southern states introduced poll taxes to disqualify black citizens from voting. For this reason poll-tax restrictions on voting in Federal elections were banned by the Twenty-Fourth Amendment of 1964.

In Britain the poll tax was introduced to replace taxes on housing as a method of financing local government. Whereas the tax on housing had varied according to the value of a family's property, so that better off people paid more, the poll tax was the same for everyone who lived in a particular area, no matter what their income. This meant that it was a regressive tax; it effectively took a much higher proportion of poor people's incomes than of rich people's. For this reason the tax was widely seen as unfair and was intensely unpopular, with many people refusing to pay it. Such evasion reduced revenues from the poll tax and meant that tax rates had to be higher, further increasing discontent. On March 31, 1990, a demonstration against the poll tax in central London turned into a violent riot that caused considerable damage to shops and other buildings. Partly as a consequence of the continuing unpopularity of the tax, Margaret Thatcher resigned as prime min-

Who really pays for taxes?

Opponents of individual taxation sometimes contend that all taxes could be levied on corporations and other businesses, rather than on individual citizens. Since some 11 percent of all Federal taxes raised in the United States in 1998 was paid by corporate income tax, it might seem that increasing such a tax on business could indeed lessen the burden on individuals. However, it might be argued that such a policy would not have the desired effect. It is often overlooked that all taxes, no matter whether they are collected from citizens or from businesses, are ultimately paid by individuals or households. The burden (or incidence) of taxation—who really bears the cost of paying it—is independent of who actually physically pays the money to the government.

Figures 1–4 are supply and demand diagrams that explain this using a tax on gasoline as an example. Figure 1 shows the market for gasoline in the absence of any form of taxation. The downward-sloping demand curve and upward-sloping supply curve meet at E, where the quantity sold and the price are Q_E and P_E respectively. Consumer surplus—the amount by which consumers value a product over and above what they pay for it—is the area A, and producer surplus—the excess of revenue received by the supplier over the minimum amount they would accept to maintain that same level of supply—is the area B.

In Figure 2 the government taxes suppliers of gasoline the sum of t cents for every gallon they sell. Although consumer preferences and thus the market demand curve are unchanged, producers feel as though demand has shifted down vertically by t cents, since they now keep t cents less for each gallon they sell. The quantity sold is Q_T, and the government collects tax revenue equal to area T. Notice that there are now two prices for gasoline: the demand price is the price consumers must pay for each gallon of gasoline; the supply price is the amount suppliers keep from each gallon sold. Figure 2 shows that demand price = supply price + tax (t).

Figure 3 portrays the effects of a tax on

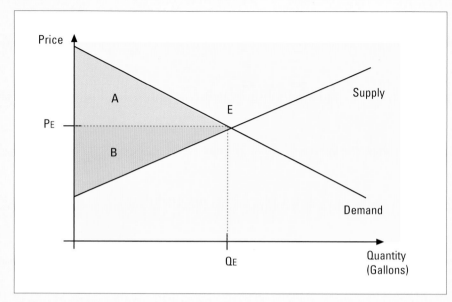

Figure 1 *The market with no tax.*

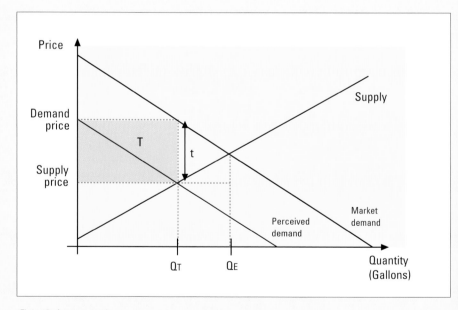

Figure 2 *A tax on producers.*

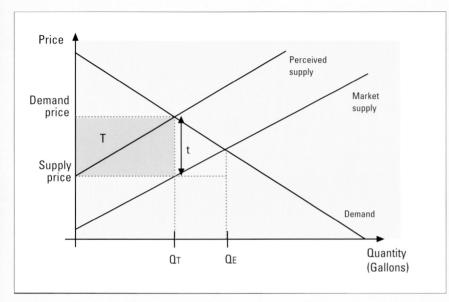

Figure 3 A tax on consumers.

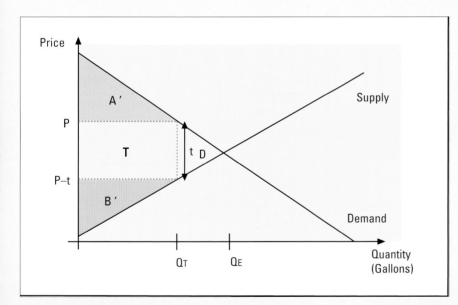

Figure 4 The tax from an economist's perspective.

consumers. They must now pay more to buy the same supply, so they feel that the supply curve has shifted up vertically by t cents. Notice that Figure 2 and Figure 3 are essentially identical—it makes no difference which curve we perceive as moving relative to the other—the resulting effect is the same.

Thus the tax can be analyzed as in Figure 4, where the person or firm that physically pays the tax—producer or consumer—is not specified. The government has gained tax revenue T, but consumers now have the smaller surplus A' and producers the smaller surplus B'. The tax has driven a wedge of size t between the supply and demand prices, and this price difference has created a deadweight loss—a loss in social welfare—the size of area D. None of these changes—in the quantity, price, producer and consumer surplus, and the deadweight loss—alters the identity of the person or body that actually delivers the tax to the government.

Firms that supply gasoline bear some of the burden of this tax in their reduced producer surplus or rents—from the area A to the smaller area A'. These firms are owned by their shareholders, whose shares reflect the value of the firms' profits and rents. Thus their shares fall in value when the tax is levied, and shareholders bear the burden of the lost producer surplus. Consequently, the whole burden of the tax is effectively borne by individuals or households, whether they are gasoline consumers, oil company shareholders, or both. Companies thus do not themselves bear the burden of taxation. One implication of this is that arguments over taxation—such as whether employers or workers should pay payroll taxes—are pointless in that imposing per-employee taxes on firms typically results in firms paying lower wages—the workers ultimately bear the burden of the tax. However, it might be that different individuals or households bear the burden of the tax depending on how it is levied. A tax on business, for example, might result in the corporation shareholders bearing the burden, rather than the workers.

ister on November 21, 1990. The poll tax was replaced by a new tax that related to the value of a homeowner's property. Ironically, the same areas of London damaged in 1990 had also been damaged by a revolt against another poll tax as early as 1381.

Reasons for taxation

There are numerous purposes for which governments may raise taxes. One of the most important is to pay for public goods. A public good is defined as something of which any person's consumption does not reduce the amount left for anyone else and which people cannot be prevented from consuming for free. In economic terms such a good is described as being nonrival in consumption and nonexcludable. National defense and lighthouses are examples of public goods. Many other goods, such as national parks, roads, libraries, and computer software, are largely nonrival in consumption because any individual's use of them does not reduce the amount left for anyone else, but they are not nonexcludable because people may be excluded from them.

The efficient price for nonrival goods is zero because additional consumption of them does not impose any additional cost on society. However, private companies typically will not supply goods at a price of zero because they cannot make a profit on them. This situation is sometimes referred to as the "tragedy of the commons," in which goods that are wanted are not supplied by markets because no individual can profit from supplying them. If private business will not supply such a good, governments traditionally do so, and so they often raise taxes to finance the supply of nonrival goods. People often disagree on which goods a government should supply purely for reasons of economic efficiency rather than for political purposes. Some people regard public libraries, for example, as an unnecessary luxury for which individual consumers, rather than the government, should pay. Although most people would accept that organizations such as police forces and customs services are necessary in any society, they nevertheless argue about how large these services should be and the precise level of funding they require. The example of computer software, meanwhile, is a reminder that governments do not supply all nonrival goods. Elements of the private sector are being introduced into the provision of many public services.

BELOW: The U.K. community charge or "poll tax"— which was brought in by Premier Margaret Thatcher in 1989—was one of the most unpopular revenue-raising measures in history. It led to unprecedented ill-feeling and riots in London.

U.S. federal income tax in 1998

Taxable income	Marginal tax rate
Up to $25,350	15.0%
$25,350–$61,400	28.0%
$61,400–$128,100	31.0%
$128,100–$278,450	36.0%
Above $278,450	39.6%

Source: Internal Revenue Service
Note: These are the rates for someone whose filing status is single.

Suppose a single individual had exemptions and deductions of $4,650, or a total income $4,650 more than taxable income. If this individual's total income were $20,000, the marginal tax on each extra dollar earned would be 15 cents or 15%. The average tax rate, however, would be:

$0.15 \times (20,000-4,650) / 20,000 = 0.115$ or 11.5%

Were the same individual to earn $300,000, it would be possible to work out her or his total tax from the table of rates to be $95,391.90, for an average tax rate of 31.8%.

Corrective taxation

Another common purpose for which governments use taxes is to correct prices in markets when these prices are inefficient. For example, the price of gasoline or road space might be considered inefficiently low if their consumption imposed costs on society that were not included in their market price or otherwise paid for. Drivers do not pay the residents of busy streets for the pollution their cars emit, nor do they pay each other for the congestion they create. By imposing taxes on gasoline and road use, however, the government can raise their prices to cover such costs and thus reach a socially efficient level. This theory of corrective taxation was developed by British economist Arthur Pigou (1877–1959) in the early 20th century, and such taxes are known as "Pigovian taxes." An example of a Pigovian tax is the toll on vehicles crossing the George Washington Bridge from Fort Lee, New Jersey, to upper Manhattan. A toll is levied in this direction but not for traffic entering New Jersey. This is because the costs of traffic congestion are estimated to be higher in Manhattan than they are in New Jersey.

A third government use of taxation is to redistribute income, perhaps from the rich to the poor or from one societal group, such as consumers, to another, such as farmers. Such redistribution is one of the most controversial purposes of taxation. Some people

object to income redistribution as a type of socialism that deprives the well-off of their incentive to make more money as well as encouraging laziness among society's worst-off members. Most countries, however, have accepted that a certain amount of wealth redistribution is necessary. They redistribute income from rich to poor by taxing the rich more heavily and by spending the revenue they raise on welfare and subsidized housing that benefit the poor. Social insurance programs such as Social Security and Health Insurance often redistribute to the poor, though by providing pensions and childcare benefits, they also redistribute wealth from one generation to another. Redistribution is built into most income taxes through their progressive structure (*see* Government and the individual, page 28).

Personal income tax

The most familiar tax to most people—and the tax that most directly affects them—is the personal income tax, which is paid on wages and salaries. It is typically a progressive tax, taking a higher percentage of a worker's income the higher that income is. Tax rates are typically expressed either as percentages or as a number of cents per dollar. With a 15 percent tax rate, for example, the government would take 15¢ of every dollar earned by a worker.

ABOVE: These special gauges at the Jack Daniel's distillery in Lynchburg, Tennessee, are used to measure the amount of whiskey being sold and thus enable the firm to keep a close watch on the amount it will have to pay in tax.

Every citizen has the right to earn a certain amount of untaxed income, or a tax allowance, which is the same for everybody. All earnings above that threshold, however, are subject to taxation, and rates of tax increase as the income of the individual increases. Such rates are sometimes called marginal tax rates because they apply to every additional dollar of income. Economists also sometimes refer to what they call the average tax rate, which is the total tax paid divided by total income. Apart from the case of a proportional tax, which taxes all income at the same rate, marginal and average tax rates will nearly always be different.

U.S. income tax returns

In the United States, for example, an individual or a married couple filing an income tax return must first calculate his, her, or their "taxable income." It is the filer's entire annual income, either in terms of wages, a salary, or profits for a self-employed person, minus any deductions to which they are entitled. They would typically include business expenses and charitable donations that are not subject to tax. Filers also deduct any relevant exemp-

tions, which can typically be claimed for having dependent children. The taxable income that remains is then subject to tax at a succession of increasing marginal rates (see box on page 85). Thus personal income tax in the United States shares characteristics in common with that in many other countries.

The system of exemptions and increasing marginal rates means that the income tax is progressive, and thus richer people pay a higher proportion of their incomes in tax than poorer people. Also, since the income tax is progressive, average tax rates are always lower than marginal tax rates.

Deadweight losses caused by taxation

Taxes usually result in deadweight losses. They are costs of a tax to consumers or producers in excess of the revenue actually raised by the tax. Deadweight loss arises when people are induced to buy or sell more or less of a good because of a tax, or perhaps because of a legal restriction such as a minimum wage. In such cases economists say that taxes or regulations have "distorted" behavior. Since rational people choose how much to buy, for example, by considering whether they value

ABOVE: A lighthouse warns ships to keep away from rocks. As such, it is an outstanding example of a public good—something from which one person may benefit without preventing anyone else from benefiting as well.

the marginal unit as much as its price, taxes that change prices at the margin relevant to consumers may distort behavior.

The deadweight loss of a tax can be demonstrated by using the example of the Social Security payroll tax in the United States. In 1998 it was a tax of 12.6 percent on labor income, half of which was paid by the employer. Because a worker earning $30,000 per year faces a marginal payroll tax of 12.6 percent, he or she may be induced to work fewer hours or to switch to a less demanding job. Such distorted behavior would create a deadweight loss because, beyond the taxes workers pay, there is an excess cost to society from their reduced work effort. However, the payroll tax does not apply to every dollar of income. In 1997 the tax applied only to the first $65,400 earned that year. Beyond this level of earnings the marginal payroll tax rate was zero. Thus for people with high wage earnings the Social Security payroll tax is a rare example of a tax that causes no deadweight loss.

Taxes and stabilization of the economy

Economists argue vigorously about whether taxes can be an effective way for governments to stabilize the economy. The theory is a central tenet of Keynesianism, introduced in the 1930s by British economist J.M. Keynes. Many contemporary economists, however, argue that government attempts to stabilize

RIGHT: Vehicles crossing the George Washington Bridge in New York may or may not have to pay a toll depending on their destination. Road tolls like this are an example of corrective or Pigovian taxation.

BELOW: Protesters demonstrate against moves by Congress to cut Social Security.

87

Taxes and tariffs

A tariff is a tax imposed on imports. Some economists take the view that it is highly desirable to raise the levels of tariffs and consequently reduce the level of taxes such as income tax. They argue that this would effectively place more of the tax burden on foreign individuals and companies and less on American citizens. In fact, however, it is highly unlikely that this would be the case, as shown by Figures 5 and 6, which analyze a tariff on imported farm machinery. This example assumes that the importing or home country, which levies the tariff, is small relative to the world market for this good and thus cannot significantly affect the price of the machines in world markets either by increasing or reducing the number of machines it buys.

Figure 5 shows the market for farm machinery before the tariff is introduced. Domestic demand for machinery slopes downward, and domestic supply slopes upward because domestic suppliers producers more machines as prices rise. Since any number of machines may be bought at their price on world markets, or P_W, this will be their price on domestic markets also. Domestic market equilibrium is at E, where quantity Q_D of machines is produced domestically, and quantity I is imported. Consumer surplus is area A and producer surplus area B.

Figure 6 shows the market once a tariff of t per machine has been levied. Since some machines are still imported, their domestic price is now P_W+t, the world price plus t, and market equilibrium is at E_T. Notice that E_T is to the left of E, meaning that fewer machines are bought in the home country. The quantity of

imports is now much smaller, at I'. Government revenues T equal the tax on imports multiplied by their quantity and are also fairly small. Domestic producers gain substantially from the tariff, however. Their producer surplus has grown from area B to the much bigger area B' because the domestic price of machines has risen. Domestic consumers, on the other hand, have lost heavily. Not only have the tax revenues T come from what was previously their surplus; but also, since domestic prices of machinery have risen, much of their surplus has been transferred to domestic producers. The tariff has also created the deadweight loss areas D_1 and D_2, also subtractions from consumers' surplus.

This example shows that if the home country is small in relation to world markets, the costs of the tariff are paid not entirely by foreigner individuals and producers, but substantially by domestic consumers. Home producers, however, gain from the tariff through being able to sell more machinery at a higher price. In fact, their gain is likely to be much larger than the revenue collected from the tariff by the government.

However, in the home country the producers' gain is the consumers' loss. They can buy less machinery than before and have to pay a higher price. Consumers have also lost surplus in the form of deadweight loss—a pure waste from society's perspective. Domestic producers often argue for tariffs, claiming that they would hurt only foreigners. Economists, meanwhile, maintain that the effects on domestic consumers reveal that this argument—though frequently seductive— is actually false.

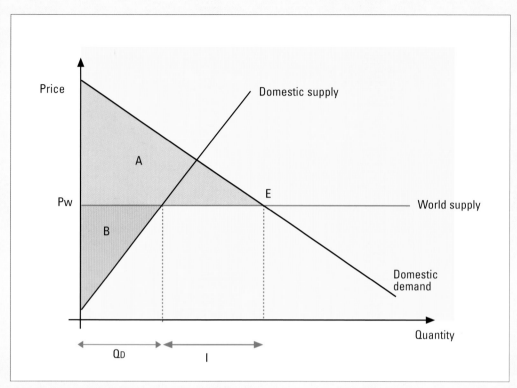

Figure 5 The market for farm machinery without a tariff.

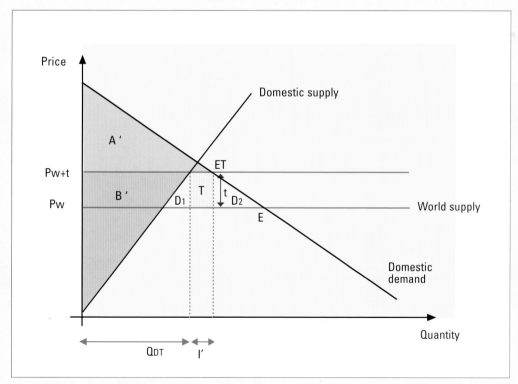

Figure 6 The market with a tariff.

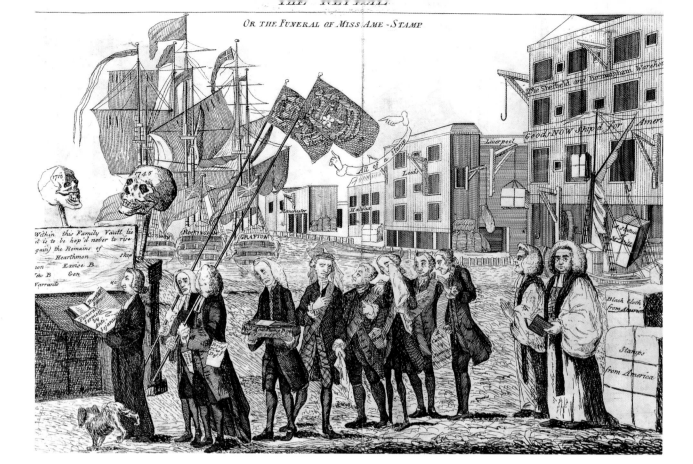

THE REPEAL
OR THE FUNERAL OF MISS AME-STAMP

the economy have actually had the opposite effect, leading to the alternating boom and bust of the trade cycle.

Circular process

During the Great Depression of the 1930s many governments were looking for ways to increase their Gross Domestic Product (GDP), the total output of their economies. Keynes, in his *General Theory of Employment, Interest and Money*, published in 1936, suggested that if governments maintained their spending but cut taxes, thereby running deficits or going into debt, consumers would spend more because they would be left with more of their income after tax. Consumers' extra demand for goods would then induce firms to produce more goods, hiring more workers in the process. These additional workers would spend their new incomes, again increasing demand for goods. By this circular process the government's original tax cut would have a "multiplied" effect on output in the economy. If total demand for goods rose beyond the economy's capacity to produce them, however, prices would rise, causing inflation.

Keynes theorized that exactly the same process would work in reverse: a rise in taxes, which with unchanged spending would imply a government surplus, would reduce consumer demand for goods, reducing employment and thus demand still further. Either the total amount of output in the economy would be reduced, or there might be a reduction in the rate of inflation, or both. Thus Keynes's

theory implied that by varying the total amount of taxation levied on the economy, governments had the power to stabilize the levels of prices and output.

The theories of Milton Friedman

Keynes's theories gained widespread acceptance in the 1940s and 1950s throughout much of the capitalist world. In the 1960s, however, economist Milton Friedman argued that running deficits or surpluses could only affect the level of prices rather than output, and that economies tended to produce their natural or maximal amounts of output most of the time. Other economists began to criticize Keynes's assumption that lower taxes would make consumers feel richer and thus increase demand. In the 1970s economist Robert Barro argued, as David Ricardo had done at the beginning of the 19th century, that reduced taxes today will actually lead consumers to expect higher taxes in the future, so that the lifetime wealth of each individual will in fact be unaffected by any tax cut. Modern economists do not agree over how much additional spending would be induced by a particular tax cut, and there is no clear evidence to show whether any extra spending would mostly increase output or prices. Most economists agree with Keynes, however, that government deficits tend to increase output and prices, while surpluses tend to reduce them.

If the level of taxation, and thus government deficits and surpluses, affects output and prices, governments may wish to stabilize both variables, since typically people dislike

ABOVE: American protests against the 1765 Stamp Act, under the terms of which the British used taxation to the political end of muzzling their colony's press and freedom of expression.

90

slumps in GDP or wild swings in the level of prices. Governments around the time of World War II were optimistic that tax or fiscal policy could be used to maintain high GDP levels and thus low unemployment. (The word "fiscal" is derived from the Latin *fiscus*, meaning money-basket, and means "relating to the tax and expenditure of the government.") Many governments have recently become pessimistic that such policies work either because lower taxes would mostly raise prices or because governments are too slow-moving to change taxes at the right times. Some stabilization occurs automatically because of progressive income taxes, however: as GDP and incomes rise, employees find they are in higher marginal tax brackets and therefore pay more tax. Thus governments typically run surpluses during booms and deficits during slumps, even without a deliberate policy change. Progressive tax systems are sometimes referred to as an economy's "automatic stabilizers" for this reason (*see* Government and the economy, page 6).

The history of taxes in the United States

Taxation lies at the heart of U.S. history. The Revolutionary War that brought the United States into existence had its roots in what was originally a protest against taxes imposed by the British on their American colonies. The early history of the Union was dogged by controversy about the respective tax-raising powers of federal and state authorities. More recently, taxation has inspired intense debate about the limits of government interference in the lives of individuals.

During the colonial period the British parliament sought to impose taxes on its American colonies to pay for the British soldiers and judges stationed there, and also to help pay for British wars both in America and in Europe. The colonists objected to the imposition of taxes and trade regulations by the Sugar Act of 1764 and rallied behind the slogan "no taxation without representation"— if Americans were to pay taxes to the British government, then Americans should have the right to elect representatives to that government. In 1765 the hated Stamp Act imposed a tax on newspapers and legal documents, effectively taxing the expression of American opinion. Resistance to the tax spurred representatives of the colonies to gather in the Stamp Act Congress later that year. The Stamp Act was repealed in 1766 but was succeeded in the following year by the Townshend Acts, which taxed British goods imported into the colonies. The Americans bore the burden of such import tariffs, and so New England colonists protested against them. In 1770 in Boston British soldiers shot dead antitax

protesters in the so-called Boston Massacre. In 1773 Massachusetts patriots disguised as Native Americans protested a tax on tea and British authority in general by dumping tea imported by a British ship into Boston harbor. British attempts to reassert control over the colonies led swiftly to the Revolutionary War.

No effective state without taxation

Despite the antitax fervor that surrounded the Revolution, it was soon evident that a federal taxing power was necessary for law, order, and a viable economy to prevail in the new republic. The Articles of Confederation, in force from 1781 until 1788, gave Congress no power to levy taxes. Congress had difficulty raising armies to quell local rebellions and struggled to pay the debts of the Continental Congress and the states left over from the Revolutionary War. Federalists such as Alexander Hamilton advocated a constitution that would give Congress tax-raising powers. Article I, Section 8 of the U.S. Constitution of 1787 gave Congress the power "to lay and collect taxes, duties, imposts, and excises." With this power the federal government was able to raise armies, pay off in full the revolutionary debts, and having established a reputation for repaying debt, borrow more money.

Article I, Section 9 of the Constitution, meanwhile, limited the tax-raising power of Congress by specifying that "No capitation, or other direct tax shall be laid, unless in proportion to the census." Members of the Convention could not, however, agree on the definition of a "direct tax." Further debate concerned the electoral and tax status of slaves. Article I, Section 9 ensured that if slaves were to be counted as part of states' populations for the assignment of Congressional seats,

ABOVE: The Boston Tea Party, one of the most famous incidents in the American struggle for independence from the British, took place on December 16, 1773, when patriots disguised as Mohawks threw 342 chests of tea into the harbor. The colonists were protesting the tax imposed on tea.

they should also count toward states' tax burdens. The infamous "three-fifths clause" of Article I, Section 2 established that slaves should count as three-fifths of a person for the purposes of both Congressional representation and direct taxation.

The Whiskey Rebellion

Between 1789 and the outbreak of the Civil War in 1865 most federal taxes were raised through tariffs or import taxes. In 1791, however, Secretary of the Treasury Alexander Hamilton persuaded Congress to impose a tax on domestically produced distilled spirits, including whiskey. Whiskey distillers, concentrated in western Pennsylvania, bore the brunt of this tax and protested violently in the Whiskey Rebellion of 1794. Although President George Washington used the government's tax-raising powers to fund troops to suppress this rebellion, all "internal" or non-tariff taxes were abolished by President Thomas Jefferson in 1802. Though the distinction between internal and external taxes has little meaning for economists, the story of the whiskey tax is a reminder that all taxes are influenced by political forces.

Tariffs on iron, woollen, and cotton goods were used not only to raise revenue but also to subsidize Northern U.S. industries as they began to compete with their British rivals. This subsidy from tariffs was effectively paid by domestic consumers, however, and Southern politicians criticized taxes that raised

the price of manufactured goods. The 1828 tariff was dubbed the Tariff of Abominations in South Carolina, and tariff policy caused much friction between Northern and Southern states before the Civil War.

In order to finance the Civil War, the Union issued large amounts of new debt by selling bonds. Bondholders had to be convinced, however, that the federal government had enough taxes at its disposal to repay the bonds. To reassure them, the government passed many new taxes, including, in 1861, the first federal income tax. It lasted only until 1872, and a revived income tax was declared unconstitutional in 1895. Nevertheless, further federal income taxes were enabled by the Sixteenth Amendment in 1913. A federal income tax was reestablished that same year and expanded during both world wars. By the end of World War II personal income tax was largely accepted in America not as an emergency measure but as part of everyday life. Almost as significant was the introduction of the Social Security payroll tax in January 1937. Payroll tax rates have only increased, while income tax rates have both risen and fallen according to the politics of the government in power.

In federal countries such as the United States individual states raise income by taxing individuals and corporations. Some may tax all income arising in the state, whether received by residents or nonresidents, while others tax all income received by residents, even if the source is outside state borders.

ABOVE: One of the lasting consequences of the American Civil War (1861-65) was income tax. This was because the Union war effort was financed largely by the sale of bonds that were underwritten by money levied in taxation.

SEE ALSO:

• Volume 2, page 48: Finance and accounting

• Volume 2, page 100: Market failure and externalities

• Volume 5, page 38: Externalities and government policy

• Volume 5, page 41: Free trade and protectionism

• Volume 5, page 107: Taxation, taxes, and subsidies

• Volume 6, page 22: The emergence of Europe

Pensions and insurance

Though pensions and insurance are different goods, the basic reason for them is the same: they require payment now for financial return in the future. The average American will spend more than a quarter of his or her life in retirement—it is essential to be financially prepared for this.

Pensions are a kind of saving, a reduction in consumption today so that more can be consumed in the future. Insurance involves making a payment today so that should something bad occur some time in the future, consumption will not have to fall too low. Though pensions and insurance are different goods, the basic reason they are wanted is the same: people like to consume similar amounts of goods and services over time. Economists say that people like this because they like to smooth their consumption.

Pension theory

If you had a fixed amount of money to spend in a week, would you prefer to buy seven meals on Friday, leaving no money for food through the rest of the week, or would you rather buy only one meal a day so that you could eat daily? There is no right or wrong answer to this question, but empirically most people prefer to spread their expenditure on food and eat about the same amount each day. To explain such choices, 19th-century economists, such as Jeremy Bentham and John Stuart Mill, developed the theory of "utility," which states that marginal utility is always positive but declining. That is to say, people always prefer more food to less, but the extra utility—i.e., the sense of well-being—conferred by the next mouthful is always less than that conferred by the present one.

People who save in pension accounts have this thinking in mind, except that they wish to save today so that they may consume when they have retired and no longer earn a wage. Life expectancy at birth in the United States in 1997 was estimated by the National Center for Health Statistics as being 73.6 years

BELOW: The theory of "utility" states that the sense of well-being conferred by the next mouthful is always less than that conferred by the present one. In this photo a diner in Wellsboro, Pennsylvania, enjoys his most satisfying mouthful.

for men and 79.2 years for women, while the typical age of retirement was calculated in 1997 by Gruber and Wise as 62 for men and around 60 for women. Thus men and, particularly, women have good reason to save money during their working lives so that they can continue to consume during their retirements. The predictable lack of earnings when old is called the "life-cycle motive" for saving. As life expectancies continue to increase, this life-cycle motive will get stronger.

Insurance theory

Insurance, in effect, spreads risk. In this way loss by an individual is compensated for at the expense of those who insure against it. In this context "risk" is an event with a known probability of outcome. An uncertain event, on the other hand, has no prior probability distribution on which to base one's expectation of the result.

The desire for insurance can be explained, as shown in Figure 1, again in accordance with the theory of utility: the utility curve is always positive but decreasing in rate. Imagine you are a householder. Tomorrow there is some probability that your house will burn down. In this case you would need to buy a new house, which would reduce your wealth and thus the amount you could consume tomorrow and after. This uncertainty about what may happen makes your wealth tomorrow risky.

Suppose your wealth if there is no fire is $100,000 and that houses are worth $60,000, so that if there is a fire and you have no insurance, then your wealth reduces to $40,000. If you had the utility curve shown in Figure 1, you would prefer to look forward to a certain

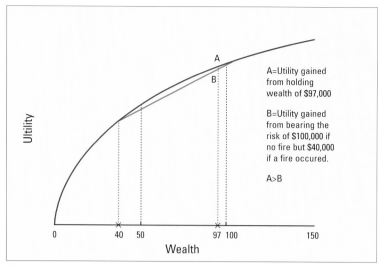

A=Utility gained from holding wealth of $97,000

B=Utility gained from bearing the risk of $100,000 if no fire but $40,000 if a fire occured.

A>B

Figure 1 A houseowner's expected utility when there is a fire risk.

level of wealth and future consumption, even when this happened to be lower than $100,000 compared with the risk of losing $60,000. If the probability of a fire is 5 percent—so the likelihood of no fire is 95 percent—then your expected utility with this risk would be less than you would receive from the certain wealth of $97,000. So if an insurer offered to pay you $60,000, the price of your house, in the event that it burned down, you would be happy to pay at least $3,000 today in return for this promise. With wealth amounting to $97,000 whether your house burned down or not, you would be happier than if you were bearing the risk. When people have declining marginal utility, they dislike risks, or are risk-averse. In this exchange the householder pays the insurer to hold the risk of the fire.

LEFT: An insurance company is happy to bear the risk of an insured house catching fire because the large amount of money at its disposal means that at worst, i.e., if the house burns down, then the company's "marginal utility" barely diminishes.

How can an insurance company be happy to bear this risk when the householder did not want to bear it? In the first instance the law of large probability allows insurance companies to say with statistical certainty what their expected payout will be for insurance. In addition, there is a difference between the householder and the insurer relating to the marginal utility of money. Indeed, insurance companies have very large amounts of money, and so for what are to them relatively small risks like house fires, their marginal utility barely diminishes. Thus their utility increases almost as a straight line with wealth, as in Figure 2 (right). Here we use the principle that a very small segment of a curve is approximately a straight line.

The insurance company starts with a large amount of wealth (W). The householder pays $3,000 for the promise of insurance, but with probability 0.05 that the insurer will pay out $60,000 to the householder. The insurer does not mind that its wealth tomorrow is risky; it is approximately risk-neutral. Further, the risk aversion that prompted the homeowner to buy insurance and the desire for a smoothing of consumption over time that necessitates saving for retirement both stem from the diminishing marginal utility of consumption.

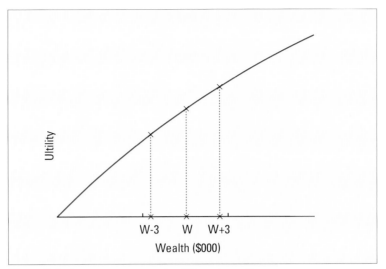

Figure 2 An insurance company's utility and wealth.

Saving for a pension

We have seen why savers wish to accumulate wealth that they are able to consume after their retirement. But how much should they save? The answer depends on the age they expect to retire, how long they expect to live, the cost of healthcare, whether they have family for whom they wish to provide, and the rate of return they expect on their savings.

Most savers attempt to get this difficult calculation only roughly right. Banks or other savings companies offer advice; still, economists are often surprised by how little many people save. Poorer and less-educated people often save only a tiny fraction of their incomes, so have few assets when they retire. At worst, many poor people have no choice and have to spend their entire incomes on survival. These people will have to rely on others during retirement. Others decide only when they are close to retirement that they have not saved enough, then scramble to build up assets. In 1981 Individual Retirement Accounts (IRAs) were created in the United States to encourage people to save more.

BELOW: Economists are often surprised at how little many people save for their retirement. Unlike this couple going yachting in Florida, many less-educated people often save only a tiny fraction of their incomes and so have very few, if any, assets when they retire.

Charles Ponzi and his pyramid scheme

A famous fraudster in the savings area of finance was the Italian Charles A. Ponzi, who in 1920 took a total of $20 million from around 40,000 people in Boston, Massachusetts. Ponzi operated a "pyramid" scheme—as new savers paid into his scheme, he gave some of that money to savers who had invested earlier. When they announced they had received a 50 percent return on their savings in only 45 days, others stampeded to lend him their money too. He claimed to be buying European postal coupons, but an investigation showed this to be largely false. People started to withdraw money from his scheme, and soon it went bankrupt, with many savers losing everything, since he had either spent their money or given it to earlier savers. He was convicted of fraud and larceny, and spent the next 14 years in jail.

Similar pyramid schemes were created in Albania and Russia after the fall of Communism. Here again, inexperienced savers were defrauded in large numbers by criminals who claimed to be using the money to build businesses but were in fact paying some of it out to earlier savers and stealing the rest. During the 1980s and '90s various false investment schemes have become popular as chain-letter and e-mail scams.

Portfolio choice

What types of wealth should savers accumulate? Individuals have a wide choice of places in which to store their assets so that they may increase in value. Savers may deposit money in a bank savings account, receiving the bank's guaranteed interest rate on what they deposit. They may buy government bonds, which would pay more interest but whose return is slightly more risky, since the value of bonds can fall as well as rise. Savers can buy shares in companies on stock markets, which tend to pay a much higher average rate of return, but which are riskier still. They may buy a house and rent it out, producing a flow of rental income. Or they may buy oil paintings or antiques in the hope that such assets will become more valuable later on.

LEFT: After the fall of communism in 1989 pyramid schemes were widespread in Russia and Albania, and many people were defrauded of their savings. Here, a violent demonstration takes place in Tirana, the capital of Albania, urging the government to compensate victims.

All these and many other assets serve the function of transferring wealth into the future. In choosing which investments to collect in their portfolio (a saver's collection of assets) savers must consider the likely average return on this portfolio. They must pay particular attention to what is known as the return's variance—the difference between the lowest rates of interest yielded by their safest investments and the risk involved in their higher yielding and more attractive assets—and try to strike a balance between the two. Economists advocate holding a mixture of many different assets (universally known as a "diversified" portfolio), since even if some lose value, others will gain, and the value of the total portfolio will be fairly stable. It was for analysis of the question of the best portfolio choice that American economist James Tobin was awarded the Nobel Prize in 1981. When asked by a reporter in an interview what his work revealed about portfolio choice, Tobin replied, "Don't put all your eggs in one basket!"

Protecting your investment

A significant concern of savers is a desire to avoid putting their savings into schemes that are unacceptably risky or even fraudulent. After all, someone who advertises shares for sale in a firm may have no such firm, intending simply to abscond with the savers' money. A good way of discerning whether a scheme is fraudulent is to examine the promises it makes. A bank may be able to guarantee a return of 7 percent per year, and some stock may rise in

value by 30 percent or more in a particular year. But any scheme that guarantees a return of 30 percent per year is likely to be extremely risky or fraudulent—such returns can be obtained only by assuming considerable risks.

In the United States the Securities and Exchange Commission (SEC) has the job of catching such fraudsters. It employs many researchers to scrutinize advertisements in newspapers and on the Internet for signs of fraud. Still, every year gullible savers have their savings stolen by people who promise them fantastic returns on their money.

Pension funds

Some savers delegate the task of choosing a portfolio of assets to someone else. To do this, they contribute to a pension, which may be operated by their employer, a bank, or another financial institution. The savings that such employees pay into their pensions form a large portfolio, which is controlled by a pension-fund manager aided by a team of researchers, who are often called institutional investors. Because the fund manager is experienced in dealing in stocks and bonds, and has a lot of information about companies in many markets, many savers feel that the fund manager will get a higher return on their money than they could themselves and so will entrust them with their savings .

Some pensions offer a "defined benefit," namely, a guarantee that savers will receive specified sums of money in the future. If the stocks and bonds that the fund manager has

ABOVE: An aging population in the U.S. has led to a greater choice in pension investment that has allowed people to make decisions about what they want to do in retirement and purchase an appropriate plan at the appropriate time of their lives. These participants in a mature exercise class in Boise, Idaho, seem to have plenty of living left to do.

An example of a pension fund— The California Public Employees' Retirement System

The California Public Employees' Retirement System (CalPERS) is a large pension fund that handles the assets of over one million Californian state and local employees. In 1999 CalPERS controlled more than $150 billion in assets. In May 1999 it held 1.4 percent of these assets in cash, 26.9 percent in bonds, 66.9 percent in stocks, and 4.8 percent in real estate. Of the total, 11.0 percent was held in California, 66.9 percent in the rest of the United States, and 22.1 percent in other countries.

CalPERS makes money for its members through the interest that is paid on its cash and bonds, the dividends that are paid on its stocks, and the rents that are paid on its real estate. It will also make money if the assets it owns rise in price. Like any pension fund, CalPERS must pay attention to the total return on its assets and any variance in this return. By owning shares in many companies, CalPERS also has voting rights to decide how these companies should be run. Therefore it must decide a policy for how it uses these votes. Further information on this example can be obtained from the CalPERS website at: <<http://www.calpers.ca.gov>>

bought rise dramatically in price, the savers' employer and the fund manager will share whatever is left over after the promised payouts have been made.

Alternatively, pensions could offer a "defined contribution," which means that the saver pays in a specified amount of money but has no guarantee of the return he or she will receive. If the assets bought rise in price, savers will get high returns; if they fall, savers will lose money. During the world stock-market rises of the 1990s many savers decided that they preferred defined-contribution pensions to defined-benefit pensions because they would allow them to share in the increasing wealth from rising share prices. Despite the increased risk, savers were pursuaded by the optimism of the rising market to take a chance and reap any possible rewards. In times of recession this is far less likely to happen.

Pensions can have many different rules, but in the background the process of building a collection of assets and later selling them for a profit and paying out the proceeds to investors is always going on.

Annuities

Many pensions offer a kind of insurance to participating savers—insurance against living to a very old age. Most people would be happy to live to the age of 100; but had they not expected to live so long, they might not have saved enough, and then they might have run out of assets at an earlier age. Pensions can insure against the uncertainty of life length by including annuities, which work in the following way.

When a saver retires, the pension wealth he or she has accumulated will be turned into a fixed sum of money per month for the rest of his or her life, however long that is. If the pensioner dies before that accumulated fund has run out, the pension fund keeps the remainder of this money and does not pay it to the pensioner's estate; if the pensioner lives longer than average and drains the accumulated fund of money invested in the annuity, the pension fund has to keep on paying out of its own spare reserves. A pension fund uses data on the ages people live to and offers pensioners a fixed sum per month that is set so that, on average, the fund does not lose by making this offer. Pension funds employ actuaries—statisticians used to making calculations involving lengths of lives—to find out how high a monthly sum they should offer.

A married pensioner might want a "joint survivor annuity." It would pay a monthly sum while either the husband or the wife is still alive. Such an arrangement allows a male pensioner, for example, to provide for his wife even if she lives much longer than him.

Annuities are such a useful form of insurance that many types of asset can now be "annuitized." Elderly homeowners can sell the rights to their home "on their death" to an insurance company. The insurance company then pays them a monthly sum until they die, whenever that is, and then sells the house, keeping the proceeds. In this case the house cannot be left to any of the children the homeowners may have had because the house is bequeathed to the insurance company.

Government social security programs

Many governments run retirement-income programs to which most wage earners are forced to contribute. This program is called Social Security in the United States, National Insurance in the United Kingdom, and the Canada Pension Plan in Canada (see Government and the individual, page 28).

The first government retirement-income program was set up for industrial workers in Germany by Chancellor Otto von Bismarck in 1889. His program was very popular with workers, for whom few pensions had previously existed; and politicians in Britain, America, and many other countries copied his example. Social Security in the United States was created in 1935 by President Franklin D. Roosevelt as part of the New Deal, which permanently established federal responsibility for disadvantaged groups. Social security systems were very popular soon after their creation, but more recently objections have been raised to them. An informed opinion of social security's merits can be gained from a good understanding of how such systems work.

Social security systems deduct some of every worker's wages each month. In the United States this deduction is called the payroll tax; in the United Kingdom it is referred to as the National Insurance contribution. Social security systems also pay money out each month to people who have

Franklin D. Roosevelt's Social Security aims:

"We can never insure one hundred percent of the population against one hundred percent of the hazards and vicissitudes of life, but we have tried to frame a law which gives some measure of protection to the average citizen and his family against the loss of a job and against poverty-ridden old age."
President Franklin D. Roosevelt on August 14, 1935, at the signing of the Social Security Act.

reached certain ages. The earliest age that social security benefits can be claimed by males is 60 in Canada, 62 in the United States, and 65 in the United Kingdom. Laws relating to social security may require older people to fulfill other conditions, such as having contributed for at least a specified number of years or having stopped working, to receive these payouts.

Some systems pay higher benefits to workers who have contributed more money during their lifetimes. Some, such as the U.K. system, pay roughly the same amount to all pensioners, while U.S. Social Security pays only slightly higher benefits to people who have contributed more. Here we see that some social security systems are in contrast to a pension because the amount that a pension pays out is usually closely related to how much an employee paid in, whereas social security is sometimes at almost a flat rate regardless of contributions. In these circumstances poorer workers, who generally have contributed less, get a better deal from social security than richer ones, presuming that they live past the eligibility age for receiving benefits. This effect is generally a deliberate social policy to help poorer people.

Social security benefits are usually paid at the same rate throughout a retiree's life. Therefore they have the annuity feature described above. They will also pay benefits to a wife or husband who lives longer than her or his spouse.

Many social security programs, including those in Germany and the United States, were designed to run much like pension funds. Employees would make contributions, which the government would then use to buy assets, selling these assets later to pay retirement benefits to the same workers. Because young employees would always be joining the system, the social security program would continue to hold a large and increasing portfolio of assets. But quickly contributors became impatient with the slow rate of benefit payments, and laws were passed (in the United States as early as 1939) to pay more benefits to early retirees. This could only be done by turning social security systems into pyramid, or Ponzi, schemes where, instead of accumulating assets, the systems paid the contributions of the young straight to retirees. This enabled higher benefits to be paid to the first retirees covered by the system than if their own contributions had been used to buy assets.

An example of someone who benefited from this arrangement was Mrs. Ida May Fuller, whose case is described in the box (below). Later generations of retirees do much less well.

Instead of their contributions having bought assets, their benefits will be paid by future generations of workers. Because workers' wages generally grow at a slower rate than the rate of return on assets, the benefits obtained by later retirees will be much lower than they would have been if their contributions had been used to buy assets.

Is social security a Ponzi scheme?

We can show that social security is a Ponzi scheme (*see* page 96) by asking the following question: Were the system to be shut down today, could it continue to pay benefits to retirees and also return to younger workers all their contributions plus interest? The answer is "no," because younger workers' contributions have already been paid to retirees. If contributions stopped flowing in, no benefits could be paid, and only some of younger workers' past contributions could be returned to them.

However, if pension-fund managers were asked the same question, they would, of course, answer "yes" about the funds they manage. They would say that they could sell some of the large portfolio of assets the fund had accumulated to return younger workers' savings with interest and use the remaining assets to pay pensions to retirees. The key difference is thus that a pension fund's assets are equal in value to its liabilities, namely, the promises of benefits it has made. Most social security plans have large unfunded liabilities, where liabilities exist in excess of the assets that a program holds.

Mrs. Ida May Fuller's experience

Ida May Fuller of Vermont was the first American to receive a monthly Social Security check, in January 1940. She was covered by the system for three years of her working life and contributed $22.54 in payroll taxes. She died at the age of 100 in 1975. Between 1940 and 1975 Mrs. Fuller received $22,888.92 in benefits. To a limited extent, Mrs. Fuller benefited from the annuity feature of Social Security because she lived longer than most women. But $22.54 would have bought only a tiny annuity. The large benefits that Mrs. Fuller received from her small contribution to the system show that Social Security works by taking contributions from the young and paying them to current retirees. For retirees who contributed for only a few years this can imply a very good deal indeed.

Social security reform

Social security systems that work like a pyramid or Ponzi scheme are termed "Pay As You Go" or PAYGO systems. Those that build up large funds of assets are termed "funded" or "prefunded" systems. In 1981 Chile created a funded social security system where workers' contributions are used to buy assets. Other countries, such as Mexico, Argentina, Australia, Malaysia, and Singapore, have imitated Chile in also creating funded systems.

In his 1998 State of the Union Address President Bill Clinton called on the U.S. Congress to "Save Social Security first." Many plans have been proposed to reform U.S. Social Security, some involving a transition from the present pyramid or PAYGO structure to a funded structure much like a private pension fund. Such a transition would require younger generations to pay twice for retirement incomes: once for older people's retirements through Social Security contributions, and once in a funded Social Security system for themselves. Perhaps due to the difficulty of persuading younger generations to pay twice, no agreement has yet been reached on how U.S. Social Security should be reformed.

Aging populations

Apart from the fact that social security plans give later retirees a much worse deal than they offer earlier retirees, the aging of the population in many countries is starting to burden their systems. During the 20th century life expectancies grew substantially in most countries, and women gave birth to fewer children than they had in previous times. As a result, the ratio of older people to young people has risen dramatically and will continue to do so. In 1950 8.1 percent of the U.S. population was aged 65 or more; in 1990 this proportion was 12.2 percent; in 2000 it stood at 13 percent; and by 2030 it is expected that 19.5 percent of the population will be 65 or older. This has implications for a vast increase in the number of persons requiring special services in areas like health, recreation, housing, and nutrition participating in entitlement programs, and requiring formal and informal care.

Since social security systems take money from the young and give it to the old, the increased ratio of retirees to workers means each worker will have to pay much more into social security to sustain benefits for each retiree at the current levels. The present projection is that payroll taxes will have to be raised or benefits cut around the year 2030 at the latest. Younger workers would dislike higher payroll taxes, which would also add to inefficiencies in labor markets, such as

ABOVE & BELOW: *During the 20th century life expectancy grew substantially in most countries. As a result, the ratio of older people to younger people has risen dramatically and will continue to do so into the 21st century and afterward.*

Driver's insurance: a deal or a steal?

It is legal to drive in the U.S. at 16 years. However, buying, owning, and driving a car legally requires quite a considerable financial investment for a teenager. For example, it is a legal requirement in most states to buy insurance to pay for damage to someone else's automobile, person, or property in the event of an accident. As a group, teenage drivers have high crash rates per mile, and 16-year-olds represent the worst in the group. Given these conditions of a considerable financial investment and the high-risk of accidents, it seems likely that insurance companies are not going to be able to issue contracts that are "actuarially fair" without expecting losses. As a result of this, auto insurance contracts usually have quite a number of "hidden" terms and conditions that will surprise the unlucky (and ignorant) teenager who has an accident.

Of course, the terms and conditions are not really hidden, but they are not always obvious to the contract holder. For example, cheaper contracts will only cover damage to someone else's vehicle and will not include damage done to your own, and there is normally a "deductible"–an amount of money that you pay in compensation before your insurance company fulfills a claim. You may be paying higher rates because the vehicle you own is expensive to repair or particularly attractive to thieves, or you may have a car whose value is hardly more than the annual cost of your insurance.

To ensure that you have appropriate insurance, it is important that you consider the following: get quotes from at least three companies, consider higher deductibles, buy a "low-profile, low-maintenance" car, take advantage of any discounts offered, e.g., low mileage, airbag, or automatic seat belts.

If you don't, then insurance companies will continue to profit from ignorance.

reducing the number of hours they work, rather than pay higher taxes (*see* Taxes, page 79). Lower benefits would, of course, be resisted by those who have retired from work. Because most Medicaid and all Medicare spending is on the old, similar problems of high healthcare costs are predicted in the 21st century and afterward. Reforming Social Security and Medicare to the satisfaction of both the old and the young will be a major challenge for the United States government and their administrators in the 21st century.

Insurance markets

The fire insurance described earlier in this chapter is an "actuarially fair" insurance contract. A contract is actuarially fair if, were the insurance company to sell a large number of similar contracts, it would make exactly zero profit. In fact, insurance companies typically make positive profits because the contracts they offer are slightly worse than actuarially fair from the buyer's perspective.

In Figure 2 (*see* page 95) the homeowner would be willing to pay slightly more than the fair $3,000—perhaps $3,200—and still have utility greater than that expected by a homeowner without insurance. In this case, if there were to be the number of house fires

that the insurer expected, it would make a profit of $200 on average from each contract it sells. Competition aamong insurance companies reduces the price of their contracts and hence the average profits they make. In order to smooth consumption, purchasers often do not pay for their insurance all at once but rather in instalments, paying regular—typically monthly or annual—premiums on their insurance policies.

Types of insurance

Insurance companies offer insurance against many risks. In most countries drivers are required to buy insurance so that they are able to pay for damage to someone else's automobile, person, or property in the event of an accident. Many people also insure their homes against fire or flood damage and their belongings against theft. In many countries workers are compelled to buy health insurance as well—though not in the United States, where in 1996 (according to the Current Population Survey published in March 1997) 16 percent of the U.S. population did not have any kind of health insurance.

In a life-insurance contract the insurer promises to pay surviving family members in the event that the insured person dies at a young age. In this way wage earners can ensure that if they were to die at a young age, their family will not be impoverished. Life insurance is often bought by people when they marry or have children because it is then that they become responsible for more family members. Businesses also buy many types of insurance—if, for example, you see a professional basketball player limp from the court, you can be sure that his or her team's management is about to file an insurance claim.

Insurance companies will not insure all risks. For example, they may not insure you against losing your wallet or failing an examination. Insurance companies worry that someone owning such insurance might become lazy, thereby raising the probability of the mishap occurring. The problem of induced laziness or carelessness is termed "moral hazard" by economists.

Insurance against heart disease is problematic for a different reason. If people know their own health status better than insurers, it will be those most at risk from heart disease who buy such insurance. Insurers will then lose money if they do not realize the risky characteristics of those insured. The tendency for insurance to be bought only by the most risky of a pool of people is termed "adverse selection," and it is one reason why governments often regulate health insurance.

Finally, some costs, like that of a hurricane hitting Miami, may be so large that no insurer could promise to pay them out. It is to deal with very large risks that insurers turn to reinsurance companies.

Reinsurance

A reinsurance company does not deal directly with homeowners or drivers, but rather shares risks that other insurers face. For example, the cost of an airplane crash may be so large that it could seriously damage—or even bankrupt—an insurance company. We can again think of this case with reference to Figure 2 (see page 95). In analyzing a small risk, we looked at a small segment of the insurer's utility function and found it roughly straight, so that the insurer was almost risk-neutral in approach. For a costlier event we must examine a bigger range of the insurer's utility function, and we would find it not straight but curving. This curved utility function implies that the insurer is risk-averse, at least for very large risks.

A "primary" insurer, which signs a contract with an airline, might buy a contract from a reinsurance company in which the reinsurer promises to pay some of the costs of any crash. Reinsurance allows insurance companies to reduce their costs—and therefore their financial risks—from any single event. Reinsurance companies do not wish to pay too much for any one event either and manage their contracts so as not to be liable for any very large costs. For this reason, even with the help of reinsurers some insurance companies, for example, will no longer sell hurricane insurance in Florida; and after a series of terrorist bombings in London in 1992 some insurers stopped selling terrorism insurance there. The risks associated were too great and not worth insuring.

RIGHT: *Though insurance companies will not insure against all risks, insuring against theft is a common home insurance.*

LEFT: *An insurance adjuster inspects a home severely damaged by a tornado in the Midwest.*

The winds of change

This chapter has discussed why most people wish to save for their retirements and insure themselves against risks. Individuals have many choices about how much to save, which assets to hold, whether to delegate the management of their assets, and how much risk they should accept. Tastes in how best to make these choices change. But the arguments for providing for old age, choosing a diversified portfolio, and insuring against risk remain strong.

In the last hundred years governments in many countries have assumed some responsibility for providing for the old. All governments are funded by taxpayers. Therefore governments and voters must think carefully about how the costs of supporting the elderly should be paid for in the coming decades. In the U.S. and many other countries this is particularly true in the light of the expected "senior boom."

Social Security vs. privatization

In January 1999 President Clinton announced a package of financial reforms in an attempt to support Social Security well into the next century. He proposed a transfer of some of the government's budget surplus in Social Security and the investment of a proportion of that money in the private sector to achieve higher returns. He also proposed the establishment of Universal Savings Accounts—a kind of government-run savings plan into which each worker would pay at source but could decide to invest as he or she chooses. Once the reform has taken place, the

President's plan would be to invest the expected surpluses from the private sector investment in military and other domestic needs.

This proposal has sparked a debate about the future of Social Security in the U.S. To some Social Security has been America's most successful social insurance program ever and should be supported and strengthened. To others, particularly more conservative voters and many representatives from Wall Street, it is not profitable enough and should be privatized.

But in reality the debate is more complicated. Defenders of the current system feel that it should not be profit related. They feel that if Social Security was privatized, then minorities and the poor would suffer, for example, women, who on average earn less and live longer than men and are therefore more likely to become impoverished during their later years. They also claim that Social Security has been largely responsible for the U.S. government's success in limiting poverty among elderly women.

Those that oppose the system, conservative think tanks, politicians, and others, are campaigning to privatize the system. They are advocating the cutting of guaranteed benefits, replacing them by forcing workers to invest in individual accounts. To back up their claims, and to show how serious they are, Wall Street interests have been investing heavily in research to show that privatization will generate profits that will offset the negative effect of the added number of people claiming Social Security in the next 30 years.

The debate continues.

SEE ALSO:

• Volume 1, page 58: Saving and borrowing

• Volume 5, page 62: Marginal analysis

• Volume 5, page 97: Savings and investment

• Volume 5, page 115: Utility

Organizations and boards

There are hundreds of organizations that facilitate economic activity in the United States by providing daily economic assistance to thousands of citizens. Some are state run, and some are nongovernmental. Both producers and consumers benefit from their services.

LEFT: The United States Treasury building in Washington D.C., which is the government department in overall charge of national revenue, taxation, and public finances.

One role governments play in the economy is to correct market failure (*see* Government and the individual, page 28). For example, government organizations are involved in the provision of public goods, environmental protection, regulating certain business activities, and even consumer protection. However, it is also the case that consumers or producers will band together in organizations to promote their own interests instead of relying solely on the government. Organizations are purposeful, structured social units made up of actual systems of cooperation where people get to-gether to carry out particular functions. Organizations shape social, political, and economic behavior; and they, in turn, are affected by these conditions.

There are numerous organizations and boards that provide daily assistance to thousands of citizens across the United States. Many of them are federal government organizations; but it is important to remember that numerous state and local agencies also exist as well as nongovernment organizations. These nongovernmental organizations (NGOs) are located in communities throughout the United States, making them more accessible to citizens who are in need of their services. They are often non-profit-making, with many of them registered as charities. They may be concerned with the environment, such as Greenpeace, or with the rights of children, such as Save the Children, or with health, with the rights of senior citizens, and so on. As central governments more or less across the globe attempt to reduce spending, these nongovernmental organizations often enter areas that government has abandoned or seriously cut back on. Since many of these organizations work together with federal government agencies, you can obtain information on them from your local town government or municipal authorities, government departments, the Internet, or your local telephone directory.

Government spending: the Internal Revenue Service (IRS)

When governments intervene in an economy, they spend money to provide certain goods and services that are underprovided, or would not be provided at all, by the market (*see* Government and the economy, page 6). In order to fund these programs, the government must collect revenue in the form of taxes (*see* Taxes, page 79). This is the responsibility of the Internal Revenue Service (IRS).

The IRS is a branch of the U.S. Government that is located within the Department of the Treasury. It is the agency responsible for the administration and enforcement of all federal tax laws except those relating to alcohol, tobacco, explosives, and firearms. It is also the agency responsible for the collection of federal taxes. Federal taxes come primarily from income tax levied on both individuals and companies. However, federal tax is not the only tax that U.S. citizens face. Additional taxes are paid to the U.S. Social Security administration, as well as to state and local governments.

Apart from tax collection and tax law enforcement, the IRS develops taxation policies and guidelines, and makes presentations to Congress. It provides information to members of the general public who have queries about whether or not they should be paying tax, if so, how much tax they should pay, and what kinds of deductions they might be eligible for due to their individual circumstances. To aid in this process of information dissemination, the IRS frequently produces publications covering these topics that are available free of charge to the public. The IRS also advises members of the public of their tax rights, responsibilities, and liabilities, and deals with any complaints that may arise. Citizens who are required to submit tax returns but fail to do so are liable to pay a fine or even face imprisonment.

As stated above, the IRS does not have any jurisdiction over alcohol, tobacco or firearms. This is the responsibility of the Bureau of Alcohol, Tobacco and Firearms. This bureau also investigates complaints concerning the contamination of alcoholic beverages or tobacco, tampering with alcoholic beverages, or firearm abuses. For further information see << http://www.irs.gov/ >>.

ABOVE: An employee processes tax return forms at the IRS service center in Ogden, Utah.

Consumer-protection agencies

Usually, consumers have limited knowledge of what they are buying before they make a purchase. It is therefore possible for consumers to buy goods and services that are defective in some way. In extreme cases injuries and illnesses could result from the use of these products. It is also possible that consumers may be unsatisfied with the after-sales service they receive, or they may feel that the terms of their sale contract agreement have not been properly upheld by the company from which they bought the product.

To prevent these kinds of risk that consumers face when purchasing goods and services, numerous consumer-protection agencies have been established. The role of these agencies is to provide consumers with vital information about products they intend to purchase and to warn consumers of the safety and health issues associated with certain products, as well as of bad business practices in the marketplace.

Federal Trade Commission: Bureau of Consumer Protection

This government agency works to protect consumers against unfair, fraudulent, or deceptive practices. It helps develop and enforce the consumer protection laws that have been passed by Congress. It also works to prevent the use of unfair and deceptive advertising and selling practices, as well as false labeling and packaging of products. As part of its activities, it investigates business practices in certain industries and may even investigate the practices of specific firms.

Firms that are found to be in violation of the consumer protection laws may be taken to court. Finally, the bureau develops educational materials and programs to educate consumers about their rights and runs programs to educate companies about good business practice and consumer-protection laws. See << http://www.ftc.gov/ftc/consumer.htm >>.

Consumer Product Safety Commission

This independent federal agency was established in 1972 to protect the public from any unreasonable risks of injury that might arise from the use of consumer products or services. Any consumer who has a complaint relating to health and safety should bring it to the attention of the commission, which may then initiate an investigation. Where injury or illness has occurred, the commission promotes research that tries to assess why product-related injuries occurred, and how they might be avoided in the future. Where products that have been marketed are found to be unsafe and expose consumers to the risk of injury, the commission will issue safety alerts to warn consumers of the danger, and may even issue a recall for that product.

The Consumer Product Safety Commission also provides a wealth of information about products on the market. It runs educational programs that not only provide information but also raise the awareness of consumers about possible hazards associated with certain products, and how they can be avoided through proper handling and use. An important part of its work involves the development of uniform standards that products must meet before being allowed on the market.

Consumer alerts and product recalls

The Consumer Product Safety Commission has the very important task of monitoring and enforcing standards for products to meet before they are released. Once a product has been released into the market, it may be recalled if a problem arises. These recalls are issued in association with the company that manufactured the product. This means that consumers who have purchased these products must return them to the place where they purchased them and receive a refund or wait for repairs to be done. Examples of a few of the recalls issued in September 1999 are listed below:

Pom-poms on certain stuffed toys—the pom-poms from approximately 472,000 stuffed toys were recalled. It was felt that they presented a health hazard since they could detach from the toys and possibly pose a choking hazard to young children who might put the pom-poms in their mouths.

Flammable spray string—approximately 912,000 cans of spray string (also known as Crazy Ribbon) were recalled. This was because the spray string cans contained flammable materials, which created a risk of burn injuries if the cans were sprayed near an open flame, such as birthday candles.

Trapeze swings—approximately 60,000 acrobatic swings that were part of a backyard gym set were recalled for repair. Bolts on the trapeze swing were exposed and caused cuts to children who played on the trapeze.

Source: Consumer Product Safety Commission << http://www.cpsc.gov/ >>.

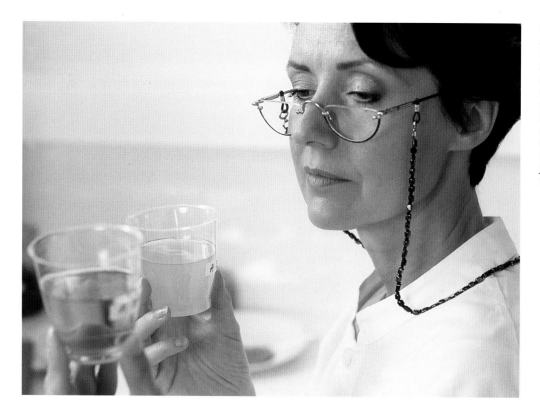

Food and Drug Administration

The Food and Drug Administration (FDA) acts in the interests of public heath and is responsible for ensuring the safety of food products, cosmetics, and medicines for human and animal consumption and use. The main job of the FDA is to ensure that these kinds of products are correctly labeled with the information that individuals need to use the products in a safe manner.

To achieve its goals, the FDA employs approximately 9,000 people to monitor the manufacture, packaging, and sale of all medical, food, and cosmetic products manufactured in the United States. This amounts to about $1 trillion worth of products, which accounts for 25 cents for every dollar spent

BELOW: The Consumer Product Safety Commission monitors and enforces standards of products such as children's toys prior to them being released onto the market.

annually by American consumers. It provides this service at a cost to each taxpayer of approximately $3 per year.

The FDA also oversees the safety of the nation's blood supply. FDA inspectors inspect blood-bank operations, check their records and labeling procedures, and check for any contaminants that might be in the blood.

Investigators and inspectors also visit and inspect over 15,000 factories each year and check that products are being correctly labeled. On occasion, they collect product samples and send them for examination by FDA scientists. Not only do scientists examine products to make sure that they are correctly labeled, but they also test samples to see whether they contain any traces of pesticides or toxic substances.

When a firm is found to be in violation of FDA regulations, the FDA will first encourage the company to rectify the problem voluntarily, or if they fail to do so, to recall the product from the market. If a company refuses to comply in this regard, the FDA can bring a legal suit against the company and force it to stop selling its product by means of a court judgment. On average, this procedure means that approximately 3,000 products a year are found to be unfit for human or animal consumption and are withdrawn from the market. In addition to this, about 30,000 import shipments a year are detained at the port of entry because the goods appear to be unacceptable. For further information see << http://www.fda.gov/ >>.

Market-regulation agencies

The activities of banks, credit unions, and trade in securities and stocks play an important role in society and contribute toward the overall financial viability of the economy. Not only is financial instability in the economy undesirable, but corruption and bad business practices that result in consumers losing money are even less desirable. Thus there are agencies that monitor these kinds of market activities.

The Federal Reserve System (FRS)

The FRS, or "the Fed" as it is usually called, is the central bank of the United States and is responsible for supervising state-chartered banks that are members of the system. It monitors the lending behavior and business practices of these banks. The Federal Reserve is also involved in the administration and development of policies concerning U.S. monetary and credit affairs.

However, the Fed also encourages public awareness of its functions and role. It develops and distributes educational materials that inform the public of its duties and activities. It also produces informational literature that advises the public on the rights and responsibilities of creditors and consumers. See << http://www.federalreserve.gov/ >>.

U.S. Department of the Treasury

This department is possibly best known for its involvement in the formulation and enforcement of tax policies, and the printing of currency and coins. However, it is also responsible for the general supervision of national banks. It becomes involved in resolving customer complaints that might arise over certain banking practices and provides a forum for consumers to air their grievances. At the same time, it is involved in developing and enforcing banking policies which ensure that banks work well and meet consumer needs. See << http://www.treas.gov/ >>.

Securities and Exchange Commission

The commission enforces federal laws that require individuals and firms involved in the trade of securities (stocks and bonds) to make certain information public. The disclosure of this information is meant to protect the public and investors who might otherwise be defrauded when trading in securities. While enforcing these laws, the commission conducts investigations into possible violations of securities law and acts to regulate the activities of investment companies, brokers, and dealers. The commission also responds to inquiries from the public relating to securities matters and will review complaints from investors who think they have been defrauded. Once an investigation is launched, if a fraud has occurred, the matter is turned over to the Department of Justice. For further information see << http://www.sec.gov/ >>.

Labor-related agencies

A large number of U.S. citizens are part of the labor force. However, the reality is that some individuals have great difficulty in finding work because some employers use discriminatory hiring practices. Other workers may find work in low-wage jobs, where working conditions are poor (*see* Government and labor, page 61). To protect workers against these kinds of situations, government agencies have been established to promote the rights and well being of workers.

Equal Employment Opportunity Commission

The Equal Employment Opportunity Commission (EEOC) was established in 1964 with the objective of ending discrimination in employment. The commission focuses on the promotion, hiring, and firing practices of firms and is responsible for enforcing federal statutes that prohibit employment discrimination. They include:
● Title VII of the Civil Rights Act of 1964. Prohibits discrimination on the basis of race, color, religion, gender, or national origin.
● The Age Discrimination in Employment Act of 1967. Prohibits discrimination against individuals who are aged 40 or older.

LEFT: *The Equal Employment Opportunity Commission was established in 1964. In 1999 it handled over 80,000 complaints about employment discrimination in the U.S.*

EEOC announces $2.1 million settlement of wage discrimination suit for class of Filipino nurses

The following excerpts, taken from a press release of the Equal Employment Opportunity Commission issued on Tuesday, March 2, 1999, illustrate how the EEOC can help workers deal with discrimination.

KANSAS CITY, MO – The U.S. Equal Employment Opportunity Commission (EEOC) today announced a $2.1 million settlement of a class employment discrimination lawsuit against Woodbine Healthcare Center (Woodbine). The suit alleged that Woodbine discriminated against 65 Filipino registered nurses in wages, assignments, and other terms and conditions of employment due to their national origin.

"This is the second significant settlement in a week that EEOC has handled dealing with discrimination against foreign-born workers," said EEOC Chairwoman Ida L. Castro. "The first, a $1.8 million settlement, brought relief to a class of agricultural workers in California and Arizona. Today's settlement stems from an instance of employees who, because of their country of origin, have been denied the dignity of working in a discrimination-free workplace that compensates them fairly. Foreign-born employees ought not be deprived of an equal opportunity to reach the American Dream."

In 1993-1995, Woodbine petitioned the Immigration and Naturalization Service (INS) to allow it to employ foreign registered nurses in its nursing home, claiming a shortage of registered nurses in the Kansas City area. Woodbine promised to employ the Filipinos as registered nurses and pay them the same wages it paid U.S. registered nurses.

However, contrary to its pledge, Woodbine paid the Filipino nurses about $6.00 an hour less than their U.S. counterparts. Moreover, rather than employing the Filipinos as registered nurses, they were assigned as nurses' aides and technicians. And even those Filipino nurses who were ultimately assigned to registered nurse jobs received lower pay than the U.S. nurses at Woodbine.

In 1996, two of the Filipino nurses filed discrimination charges with EEOC. An agency investigation found reasonable cause that Woodbine violated Title VII of the Civil Rights Act by failing to assign and compensate the Filipino nurses as registered nurses, and harassing and intimidating them because of their national origin.

Following EEOC's "cause" finding, Woodbine rejected efforts to conciliate the matter and one of the Filipino nurses, Aileen Villanueva, filed a private discrimination lawsuit. The EEOC intervened in the suit, alleging a pattern and practice of discrimination against all of the Filipino nurses at Woodbine, after the Commission's General Counsel certified that the case was of general public importance. "EEOC's intervention was instrumental in achieving a swift class settlement in this case," said Chairwoman Castro.

LEFT: Despite the Civil Rights Act of 1964, discrimination on the grounds of color continued. This demonstration, in New York City in 1970, was against the city's hiring practices for higher-paying construction jobs: it was alleged that white workers were hired rather than blacks.

● The Equal Pay Act of 1963. Prohibits discrimination on the basis of gender and upholds the principle of equal pay for equal work.

● Title I of the Americans with Disabilities Act of 1990. Prohibits discrimination on the basis of disability. The federal government is excluded from it however.

● The Civil Rights Act of 1991—includes provision for monetary damages in cases where intentional discrimination occurs.

The commission has 50 field offices located throughout the U.S. If individuals feel that they have been discriminated against, they can approach EEOC and ask it to undertake an investigation into the matter. The commission manages 75,000 to 80,000 complaints each year. If the commission finds the individual's complaint to have merit, it will first try to resolve the issue between the two parties by bringing them together to discuss the issue. However, if this method is unsuccessful in resolving the issue, then the EEOC may assist the individual in bring a lawsuit against the party that acted in a discriminatory manner. For further information see << http://www.eeoc.gov/ >>.

U.S. Department of Labor

The U.S. Department of Labor is responsible for the administration and enforcement of over 180 federal statutes that relate to labor issues. These laws cover all aspects of employment, including workplace safety, worker rights, unemployment insurance, the promotion of equal opportunity employment, and basic conditions of employment. The

BELOW: The U.S. Department of Labor in Washington, which is responsible for the administration and enforcement of the law covering all aspects of employment.

department also provides information on these regulations to the public and to companies. This is important in educating the public about fair labor practices, minimum wages, and their rights as workers.

Within the Department of Labor there are different sections that focus on specific aspects of worker issues. The Bureau of Labor Statistics is the principal agent for research into labor issues. It collects facts and figures relating to the labor market and documents wage levels and working hours across industries. This information is useful at a number of levels. On the one hand, it can be used by Congress to make decisions concerning labor legislation. However, the general public may also benefit. The bureau has an "Occupational Outlook Program" that provides career information to prospective college graduates. It offers career information for a wide range of occupational categories and documents the training requirements, working conditions, working hours, and job prospects associated with each particular career. The bureau also produces consumer publications that provide tips on how to write resumes and prepare for job interviews.

A different section within the Department of Labor focuses exclusively on workplace health and safety. The Occupational Health and Safety Administration (OSHA) was created to encourage workers and employers to work together to remove workplace hazards and improve general safety standards in the workplace. One of the main functions of OSHA has been to develop specific guidelines for workplace safety and health. These

Judge upholds OSHA citations for Houston building owner accused of using untrained workers to remove asbestos

Below, excerpts taken from a press release issued by the U.S. Department of Labor, Office of Public Affairs, on September 9, 1999, illustrate how OSHA can help in bringing cases against firms that breach health and safety guidelines.

An administrative law judge has upheld citations for wilful safety and health violations issued by the Occupational Safety and Health Administration as well as $1,136,900 in OSHA penalties against Eric K. Ho; Ho Ho Ho Express, Inc.; and Houston Fruitland, Inc., in a case involving the use of untrained workers to remove potentially dangerous asbestos.

An explosion and fire at a Houston, Tex., building on March 11, 1998, in which three workers were burned, prompted an OSHA investigation that revealed a clandestine asbestos removal project. Ho was using untrained workers, all of whom were non-English speaking, uneducated and undocumented immigrants, to remove asbestos from the building he owned.

"The Judge's decision shows that flagrant violations of the law will not be tolerated and offenders will be severely sanctioned. We must commend the courage of these Mexican nationals who come forward to tell their stories," said Ray Skinner, OSHA Houston South area director. "That they were exploited and subjected to potentially grievous injury should not be forgotten."

"The workers, who were never told they were removing asbestos or about the hazards associated with the material, were not provided with proper respiratory protection and performed the work in street clothes they wore home," Skinner said. "The employer had the employees inside a locked and fenced area removing the asbestos at night in order to avoid detection."

OSHA said that Ho was aware that the buildings contained asbestos when he purchased the site but made no serious attempt to protect his employees from this known cancer-causing substance. Ho had obtained a bid from a certified asbestos abatement contractor but chose instead to hire the Mexican nationals.

guidelines, which are binding on all firms in the United States, cover all aspects of firm safety and health. For example, the regulations specify the number of fire exits and fire extinguishers required in the workplace, the kind of safety training that workers must receive, the number of toilets that should be provided, and the acceptable noise level in the workplace. Inspectors working on behalf of OSHA regularly conduct surprise factory inspections to check whether firms are in compliance with these regulations. Firms found to be inviolation of these regulations may be issued a citation or, in more severe cases, may be fined.

OSHA also provides education on occupational health and safety issues to the private sector, as well as free consultation services for small businesses. This means that small businesses can benefit from the services of a consultant who will walk through the workplace with them and point out potential workplace hazards. For further information see << http://www.dol.gov/ >>. For information on OSHA see << http://www.osha.gov/ >>.

U.S. Social Security Administration (SSA)

While this administration is not strictly a labor agency, employed individuals pay Social Security taxes. All U.S. citizens can and should apply for a Social Security card. This is especially important for when you find a job, since your Social Security number is used as a means of keeping a record of your personal details and your earnings. When you find a job, your employer will deduct a certain amount from your wage to pay for Social Security and Medicare taxes. The employer then matches the amount that he or she deducts, and sends these taxes to the IRS, while at the same time reporting your earnings to the Social Security Administration. As you work and pay these taxes, you earn credits that make you eligible to receive certain Social Security benefits in the future.

The main benefits provided by social security to eligible (i.e., you must have earned enough credits) individuals include:

● Retirement benefits. Individuals retire at age 65 and receive income benefits.

● Disability benefits. Individuals with a disability that is severe enough to prevent them from doing work for a year or more, or if the disability is expected to end in early death, receive benefits and healthcare coverage while they attempt to work.

● Family benefits. If you are eligible for retirement or disability benefits, certain family members may also be eligible for benefits on the basis of your Social Security record.

● Survivors. If you earned enough Social Security credits while working, your family may be eligible for benefits when you die.

● Medicare. Medicare benefits are made up of two parts, namely hospital insurance and medical insurance. Individuals who are over the age of 65 and receive Social Security benefits, or individuals who have been receiving disability benefits for two years, automatically qualify for both hospital and medical insurance. Other individuals must fill in a formal application.

LEFT: A sign warning of asbestos contamination at a site in Love Canal near Niagara Falls, New York. The site was evacuated in 1978 when high levels of toxic waste were found to cause birth defects and illnesses. The EPA successfully lobbied for the establishment of a nationwide program for toxic waste-site cleanups, which was ratified by the goverment in 1980.

● Supplemental Security Income Benefits—monthly payments are made to individuals who have low incomes and who own only a few assets. To qualify for this assistance, you must be over the age of 65 or disabled. These benefits are financed out of general tax revenues.

See << http://www.ssa.gov/ >>.

Environmental agencies

Because natural resources are often not priced in the market system, there is a tendency for these resources to be exploited. This generates the need for some external agency to play a protective role in this regard. While there are many environmental groups in the United States, the federal Environmental Protection Agency (EPA) is probably the best-known agency concerned with environmental issues.

The EPA is concerned with human health and the natural environment—namely, air, water, and land—or resources on which human life depends. The EPA lobbies Congress and other bodies to take environmental considerations into account when devising legislation. It also encourages Congress to ensure that the federal laws relating to the protection of human health and the environment are in fact enforced once they have been enacted. The EPA conducts research into environmental issues and provides detailed information to government bodies, the public, and firms on environmental matters. Information provided relates to a

BELOW: An EPA agent uses analytical test paper to find out whether or not tailpipe soot contains lead.

ABOVE: A scientist from the EPA checks water for contamination at the Toolik Lake research camp, Alaska.

wide range of topics, including the impact of toxins and pesticides on human health and the environment, issues related to the safety of drinking water, acid rain, landfills, recycling, and air quality. This information is distributed by means of newsletters, press releases, and pamphlets.

The EPA runs outreach programs for industry that encourage greater awareness of environmental issues and concerns. They focus particularly on pollution levels and the ways in which firms dispose of their waste. The agency also runs an asbestos program that provides assistance to building contractors and members of the public on locating and removing asbestos. Finally, the EPA may make financial grants to projects that are aimed at protecting the environment. For example, in August 1999 the EPA gave a total of $1.1 million to the State of Maine to protect and improve the quality of Maine's water resources. The EPA also gave a grant of $150,000 to the State of Vermont to train teachers and create a curriculum that will include environmental education. For further information see << http://www.epa.gov/ >>.

U.S.—saint or sinner?

In an article entitled "What Price Riches?" that appeared in the British *Guardian* newspaper on November 11, 1999, journalist John Vidal spoke of the split personality the United States presented to the world at the start of a new millennium. On the one hand, it has been partly responsible for almost everything that has affected the global environment adversely during the last century: car pollution, genetic engineering, nuclear power, global tourism, and so on. On the other hand, the nation professes a love of nature and the environment, and has made a huge investment in the science and technology that can clear up some of the devastation for which it has been responsible.

It is widely agreed that during the 20th century the United States has always protected its own industrial interests above all others. Lobbying by major business players has led to the U.S. goverment refusing to sign the biodiversity treaty, granting drug companies the freedom to patent genetic material found mainly in developing countries, mining the Antarctic without guaranteeing protection against environmental damage, and watering down global environmental and consumer protection laws. It is also true that the U.S. has some of the highest clean-air and auto-emission standards, the most virulent antismoking laws, the most outspoken conservationists, and the most innovative technology for alternative energies. On the outcome of this debate may hang the future of life itself.

Business-related organizations and lobbying

Consumers are not the only group who have organizations promoting their interests. Producers also have organizations to promote their business interests. In particular, the U.S. Chamber of Commerce, established in 1912, is one of the largest federations of business interests in the world, representing more than 3 million U.S. companies.

The main aim of the chamber, which is not a government agency, is to promote the causes and interests of business in all spheres of society. This includes lobbying Congress for legislation that will favor business and encour-

aging policy makers to uphold free-market ideals. It lobbies government to remove restrictions and obligations placed on business by certain laws, and argue for lower corporate income taxes.

The chamber also provides services to its members. Firms that join the federation can take advantage of their research databases and the information they have collected about workplace regulations, minimum wage information, and laws governing the responsibilities of employers to their workers. The chamber provides business advice on how firms can improve their production operations and increase their profits. Finally, the chamber holds information on investment opportunities abroad for U.S. companies. With

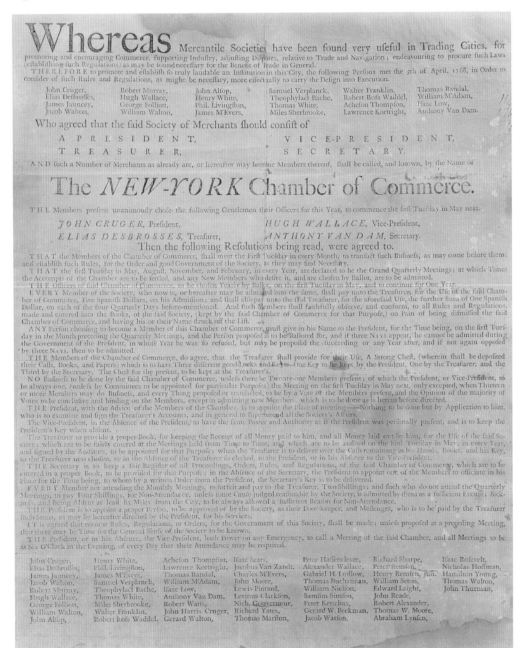

LEFT: *The charter of the New York Chamber of Commerce, drawn up in 1912. The Chamber of Commerce is an independent agency that promotes the causes and interests of business in all spheres of society.*

LEFT: *The home of the United States Chamber of Commerce in Washington.*

all these resources at hand, the Chamber of Commerce, which has local branches, is an important source of information for any business person. For further information see <<http://www.uschamber.com>>.

The Greater Dallas Chamber

A good example is the Greater Dallas Chamber, whose mission statement is "to unite and engage the Dallas region's business community and provide dynamic business and civic leadership to develop and sustain a prosperous economy and a vibrant community."

The chamber provides a huge amount of local information though all the normal media channels: research for economic development prospects, a range of publications on business and industry, labor analysis, wage and benefits surveys, statistics and data, charts, graphs, and demographics, as well as information that would assist local companies in their marketing and publicity to access the global marketplace. For further information see << http://www.gdc.org/ >>.

Lobbying firms

There are thousands of lobbying firms in the U.S., representing all areas of interest. Business lobbying normally centers around finance and the law, with lobbying firms using their contacts and expertise to further the business of their clients. For example, they may apply effectively for government grants or loans on behalf of a client, or their expertise in the law may enable a company or companies to affect government decision-making and legislation in their favor.

One such firm is New Jersey's Public Strategies Impact. It offers: "Communication. Access. Strategic Planning. Creative Problem Solving." With management staff recruited from both the Republican and the Democrat parties, the company offers "bipartisan personnel, who have a thorough knowledge of the lawmaking process in New Jersey, as well as the people who make the law." The company offers help "From government to public and community relations, media to finance, and business to law." Public Strategies Impact has a huge client list, including: AAA Autoclubs of New Jersey, the Mobil Oil Company, the New York Giants football team, Rutgers—the State University of New Jersey, and the City of Newark, as well as thousands of small local businesses. See << http://www.njlobbyist.com/service/assoc-manage.htm >>.

The effectiveness of organizations

There are many organizations that play an important role in facilitating economic activities in the U.S. economy. When they are effective, both consumers and producers benefit from their services. However, organizations sometimes do not work well, and some are less effective than others. The effectiveness of an organization will depend, among other things, on its internal bureaucracy and administrative framework, the resources it has at its disposal, and its ability to respond to the changing social, political, and economic conditions of the society in which it operates. These issues form part of the broad subject of organizational design.

SEE ALSO:

• Volume 1, page 24: Banks and banking
• Volume 2, page 10: Market failure and externalities
• Volume 5, page 62: Externalities and government policy
• Volume 5, page 93: Regulation and antitrust laws
• Volume 5, page 107: Taxation, taxes, and subsidies

Glossary

accounts records of earnings, expenditure, assets, and liabilities kept by individuals, firms, and governments.

balance of payments a record of a country's international trade, borrowing, and lending.

balance of trade an indicator of a country's financial condition produced by subtracting the value of imports from the value of exports.

balance sheet a list of assets and liabilities that shows the financial condition of a firm, individual, or other economic unit.

barter a system of trading in which goods are exchanged for other goods rather than for money

black market an illegal part of the economy that is not subject to regulation or taxation and that often deals in high-priced, illegal or scarce commodities.

bond a legal obligation to pay a specified amount of money on a specified future date.

boom and bust a phrase that describes a period of wild swings in economic activity between growth and contraction.

business cycle the periodic but irregular fluctuation in economic activity, usually measured by GDP, which rises and falls for reasons economists do not fully understand.

capital the physical assets owned by a household, firm, or government, such as equipment, real estate, and machinery. Capital is also used to mean financial capital, or money used to finance a business venture.

capitalism an economic system based on private ownership and enterprise and the free market. Capitalism has been the dominant economic system in the western world since around the 16th century.

central bank a public organization, sometimes subject to government influence but often independent, established to oversee and regulate a country's monetary and financial institutions.

commodity a primary product such as coffee, cotton, copper, or rubber. In economics, "commodity" is also used to describe a good or service created by the process of production.

communism a political doctrine based on the ideas of the philosopher Karl Marx that seeks to establish social equality through central regulation of the economic activity and communal ownership. *See also* planned economies.

comparative advantage the advantage gained by a producer—an individual, firm, or government—if they can produce a good at a lower opportunity cost than any other producer.

consumer good an economic good or commodity that is bought for use by a household rather than by industry, for example.

consumer price index (CPI) an economic indicator based on the price of a range of goods and services to calculate an average for expenditure of a U.S. family.

cost benefit analysis the appraisal of a project or policy, for example, by comparing all the social and financial costs with the social and financial benefits arising from that project or policy.

curve a line plotted between points on a graph; an economic curve can be a straight line.

deflation a general downward movement of prices.

demand the desire for a particular good or service backed by the ability to pay for it.

depression a deep trough in the business cycle, usually marked by high prices and high unemployment.

developing country a poor country that is undergoing a process of economic modernization, typically including an increase of GDP through the development of an industrial and commercial base.

economies of scale factors which cause the average cost of producing a good to fall as output increases.

entrepreneurship the ability to perceive opportunities in the market and assemble factors of production to exploit those opportunities.

externality a cost or benefit falling on a third party as the result of an economic activity which is not accounted for by those carrying out that activity.

factors of production the productive resources of an economy, usually defined as land, labor, entrepreneurship, and capital.

fiscal policy the attempts a government makes to maintain economic balance by altering its spending on goods or services or its revenue-raising through taxation.

foreign exchange rate the rate at which one country's money is exchanged for another. The rate is often used as a measure of the relative strengths and weaknesses of different economies.

free trade international trade that is not subject to barriers such as tariffs or quotas.

gross domestic product (GDP) the total value of the final output within the borders of a particular economy.

gross national product (GNP) GDP plus the income accruing to domestic residents from investments abroad, less the income earned in the domestic market by foreigners abroad.

inflation an upward movement in the general level of prices.

interest the amount earned by savers or investors on their deposit or investment or paid by borrowers on their loan. The amount of interest is determined by the interest rate.

Keynesianism an economic doctrine based on the theories of J. M. Keynes that advocates government intervention through fiscal policy to stabilize fluctuations in the economy.

labor the workforce who provide muscle or brainpower for economic activity.

laissez-faire a French term for "let it do," originally used in classic economics to describe an economy with no government intervention.

land land and all natural resources such as oil, timber, and fish.

liquidity a measure of how easily an asset can be converted into cash.

macroeconomics the name given to the study of the economy as a whole rather than with the detailed choices of individuals or firms. *See also* microeconomics.

the market an arrangement which facilitates the buying and selling of a good, service, or factor of production. In a free market the prices which result from this are regulated by the laws of supply and demand rather than by external constraints.

mercantilism an economic policy popular in Europe from the 16th to the 18th centuries that stressed the importance of exports to earn reserves of gold and silver and used high tariffs to prevent imports.

microeconomics the study of individual households and firms, the choices they make in individual markets, and the effects of taxes and government regulation. *See also* macroeconomics.

monetarism an economic doctrine that regards the quantity of money in an economy as the main determinant of aggregate demand. As such, attempts by government to increase output by stimulating demand will only result in inflation.

monetary policy the attempt to regulate inflation and economic activity by varying the money supply and interest rates. Monetary policy is often the responsibility of a central bank.

money supply the amount of liquid assets in an economy that can easily be exchanged for goods and services, usually including notes, coins, and bank deposits that can be transferred by writing checks.

monopoly a market in which there is only one supplier of a good or service for which there is no close substitute.

neocolonialism a relationship between a country and a former colony in which the business interests of the first continue to dominate the economy of the latter.

opportunity cost the best alternative that must be given up when an economic choice is made.

planned economy an economy in which production and distribution are determined by a central authority, such as a ruler or a government.

private sector that part of an economy in which activity is decided and the means of production owned by individuals or firms rather than government. *See also* public sector.

productivity the ratio between the input of resources such as capital and labor and the resulting output of goods and services.

protectionism an economic doctrine that attempts to protect domestic producers by placing tariffs on imported goods.

public sector that part of an economy owned by a government or other public bodies such as state administrations.

recession a severe contraction of economic activity marked by two successive quarters of falling GDP.

specialization the decision by an individual, firm, or government to produce only one or a few goods or services.

sustainable development a form of economic growth that seeks to use renewable rather than finite resources and to minimize the permanent damage done to the environment by economic activity.

supply the quantity of a good or service available for sale at a particular price.

taxes and tariffs compulsory charges placed on economic activity by governments. Taxes might be placed on wealth or income, on business profits, as a sales tax on transactions, or as license fees on activities such as driving. Tariffs are taxes placed on imports into a country.

trusts anticompetitive alliances formed among businesses to force prices up and bring costs down. Trusts were outlawed in the United States by the Sherman Antitrust Act of 1890.

unemployment the condition of adult workers who do not have jobs and are looking for employment.

wealth the total assets of a household, firm, or country less its total liabilities.

welfare state a system of welfare provision by a government to keep its citizens healthy and free from poverty. Welfare provisions typically include free health care, insurance against sickness or unemployment, old age pensions, disability benefits, subsidized housing, and free education.

The World's Economies, 1996

	Population (millions)	GDP $m		Population (millions)	GDP $m		Population (millions)	GDP $m
Afghanistan	20.9	12.8	Germany	81.9	2,364.6	Nigeria	115.0	27.6
Albania	3.4	2.7	Ghana	17.8	6.2	North Korea	22.5	21.5
Algeria	28.8	43.7	Greece	10.5	120.0	Norway	4.3	151.2
Angola	11.2	3.0	Guadeloupe	0.4	3.7	Oman	2.3	15.3
Argentina	35.2	295.1	Guatemala	10.9	16.0	Pakistan	140.0	63.6
Armenia	3.6	2.4	Guinea	7.5	3.8	Panama	2.7	8.2
Australia	18.1	367.8	Guinea-Bissau	1.1	0.3	Papua New Guinea	4.5	5.0
Austria	8.1	226.5	Haiti	7.3	2.3	Paraguay	5.0	9.2
Azerbaijan	7.6	3.6	Honduras	5.8	4.0	Peru	23.9	58.7
Bahamas	0.3	3.5	Hong Kong	6.2	153.3	Philippines	69.3	83.3
Bahrain	0.6	5.7	Hungary	10.0	44.3	Poland	38.6	124.7
Bangladesh	120.1	31.2	Iceland	0.3	7.2	Portugal	9.8	100.9
Barbados	0.3	2.0	India	944.6	357.8	Puerto Rico	3.7	30.3
Belarus	10.3	22.5	Indonesia	200.5	213.4	Qatar	0.6	7.5
Belgium	10.2	268.6	Iran	70.0	132.9	Réunion	0.7	2.9
Benin	5.6	2.0	Iraq	20.6	21.9	Romania	22.7	36.2
Bermuda	0.1	2.1	Ireland	3.6	62.0	Russia	148.1	356.0
Bhutan	1.8	0.3	Israel	5.7	90.3	Rwanda	5.4	1.3
Bolivia	7.6	6.3	Italy	57.2	1,140.5	Saudi Arabia	18.8	125.3
Bosnia	3.6	3.3	Jamaica	2.5	4.1	Senegal	8.5	4.9
Botswana	1.5	4.8	Japan	125.4	5,149.2	Serbia, Montenegro	10.3	15.7
Brazil	161.1	709.6	Jordan	5.6	7.1	Sierra Leone	4.3	0.9
Brunei	0.3	4.6	Kazakhstan	16.8	22.2	Singapore	3.4	93.0
Bulgaria	8.5	9.9	Kenya	27.8	8.7	Slovakia	5.3	18.2
Burkina Faso	10.8	2.4	Kirgizstan	4.5	2.5	Slovenia	1.9	18.4
Burundi	3.2	1.1	Kuwait	1.7	31.0	Somalia	9.8	3.6
Cambodia	10.3	3.1	Laos	5.0	1.9	South Africa	42.4	132.5
Cameroon	13.6	8.4	Latvia	2.5	5.7	South Korea	45.3	483.1
Canada	29.7	569.9	Lebanon	3.1	12.1	Spain	39.7	563.2
Central African Republic	3.3	1.0	Lesotho	2.1	1.3	Sri Lanka	18.1	13.5
Chad	6.5	1.0	Liberia	2.2	2.3	Sudan	27.3	10.7
Chile	14.4	70.1	Libya	5.6	23.1	Suriname	0.4	1.3
China	1,232.1	906.1	Lithuania	3.7	8.5	Swaziland	0.9	1.1
Colombia	36.4	80.2	Luxembourg	0.4	18.9	Sweden	8.8	227.3
Congo	46.8	5.7	Macau	0.4	7.4	Switzerland	7.2	313.7
Congo-Brazzaville	2.7	1.8	Macedonia FYR	2.2	2.0	Syria	14.6	16.8
Costa Rica	3.5	9.1	Madagascar	15.4	3.4	Taiwan	21.5	275.0
Cote d'Ivoire	14.0	9.4	Malawi	9.8	1.8	Tajikistan	5.9	2.0
Croatia	4.5	18.1	Malaysia	20.6	89.8	Tanzania	30.8	5.2
Cuba	11.0	18.0	Mali	11.1	2.4	Thailand	58.7	177.5
Cyprus	0.8	8.9	Malta	0.4	3.3	Togo	4.2	1.3
Czech Republic	10.3	48.9	Martinique	0.4	3.9	Trinidad and Tobago	1.3	5.0
Denmark	5.2	168.9	Mauritania	2.3	1.1	Tunisia	9.2	17.6
Dominican Republic	8.0	12.8	Mauritius	1.1	4.2	Turkey	61.8	177.5
Ecuador	11.7	17.5	Mexico	92.7	341.7	Turkmenistan	4.2	4.3
Egypt	63.3	64.3	Moldova	4.4	2.5	Uganda	20.3	5.8
El Salvador	5.8	9.9	Mongolia	2.5	0.9	Ukraine	51.6	60.9
Eritrea	3.3	0.8	Morocco	27.0	34.9	United Arab Emirates	2.3	44.6
Estonia	1.5	4.5	Mozambique	17.8	1.5	United Kingdom	58.1	1,152.1
Ethiopia	58.2	6.0	Myanmar	45.9	63.4	United States	269.4	7,433.5
Fiji	0.8	2.0	Namibia	1.6	3.6	Uruguay	3.2	18.5
Finland	5.1	119.1	Nepal	22.0	4.7	Uzbekistan	23.2	23.5
France	58.3	1,533.6	Netherlands	15.6	402.6	Venezuela	22.3	67.3
Gabon	1.1	4.4	Netherlands Antilles	0.2	1.9	Vietnam	75.2	21.9
Gambia, The	1.1	0.4	New Zealand	3.6	57.1	West Bank & Gaza	0.8	3.9
Georgia	5.4	4.6	Nicaragua	4.2	1.7	Yemen	15.7	6.0
			Niger	9.5	1.9	Zambia	8.3	3.4
						Zimbabwe	11.4	6.8

Further reading

Allen, L. *Encyclopedia of Money*. Santa Barbara, CA: ABC-Clio, 1999.

Ammer C., and Ammer, D. S. *Dictionary of Business and Economics*. New York: MacMillan Publishing Company, 1986.

Atrill, P. *Accounting and Finance for Non-Specialists*. Engelwood Cliffs, NJ: Prentice Hall, 1997.

Baker, J.C. *International Finance: Management, Markets, and Institutions*. Engelwood Cliffs, NJ: Prentice Hall, 1997.

Baites, B. *Europe and the Third World: From Colonisation to Decolonisation, 1500-1998*. New York: St. Martins Press, 1999.

Bannock, G., Davis, E., and Baxter, R.E. *The Economist Books Dictionary of Economics*. London: Profile Books, 1998.

Barilleaux, R.J. *American Government in Action: Principles, Process, Politics*. Englewood Cliffs, NJ: Prentice Hall, 1995.

Barr, N. *The Economics of the Welfare State*. Stanford, CA: Stanford University Press, 1999.

Barro, R.J. *Macroeconomics*. New York: John Wiley & Sons Inc, 1993.

Baumol, W.J., and Blinder, A.S. *Economics: Principles and Policy*. Forth Worth, TX: Dryden Press, 1998.

Begg, D., Fischer, S., and Dornbusch, R. *Economics*. London: McGraw-Hill, 1997.

Black, J.A. *Dictionary of Economics*. New York: Oxford University Press, 1997.

Blau, F.D., Ferber, M.A., and Winkler, A.E. *The Economics of Women, Men, and Work*. Engelwood Cliffs, NJ: Prentice Hall PTR, 1997.

Boyes, W. and Melvin, M. *Fundamentals of Economics*. Boston, MA: Houghton Mifflin Company, 1999.

Bradley, R.L., Jr. *Oil, Gas, and Government: The U.S. Experience*. Lanham, MD: Rowman and Littlefield, 1996.

Brewer, T.L., and Boyd, G. (ed.). *Globalizing America: the USA in World Integration*. Northampton, MA: Edward Elgar Publishing, 2000.

Brownlee, W.E. *Federal Taxation in America: A Short History*. New York: Cambridge University Press, 1996.

Buchholz, T.G. *From Here to Economy: A Short Cut to Economic Literacy*. New York: Plume, 1996.

Burkett, L., and Temple, T. *Money Matters for Teens Workbook: Age 15-18*. Moody Press, 1998.

Cameron, E. *Early Modern Europe: an Oxford History*. Oxford: Oxford University Press, 1999.

Chown, J.F. *A History of Money: from AD 800*. New York: Routledge, 1996.

Coleman, D.A. *Ecopolitics: Building a Green Society* by Daniel A. Coleman Piscataway, NJ: Rutgers University Press, 1994.

Cornes, R. *The Theory of Externalities, Public Goods, and Club Goods*. New York: Cambridge University Press, 1996.

Dalton, J. *How the Stock Market Works*. New York: Prentice Hall Press, 1993.

Daly, H.E. *Beyond Growth: the Economics of Sustainable Development*. Boston, MA: Beacon Press, 1997.

Dent, H.S., Jr. *The Roaring 2000s: Building the Wealth and Lifestyle you Desire in the Greatest Boom in History*. New York: Simon and Schuster, 1998.

Dicken, P. *Global Shift: Transforming the World Economy*. New York: The Guilford Press, 1998.

Economic Report of the President Transmitted to the Congress. Washington, D.C.: Government Publications Office, 1999.

Elliott, J. H. *The Old World and the New, 1492-1650*. Cambridge: Cambridge University Press, 1992.

Epping, R.C. *A Beginner's Guide to the World Economy*. New York: Vintage Books, 1995.

Ferrell, O.C., and Hirt, G. *Business: A Changing World*. Boston: McGraw Hill College Division, 1999.

Frankel, J.A. *Financial Markets and Monetary Policy*. Cambridge, MA: MIT Press, 1995.

Friedman, D.D. *Hidden Order: The Economics of Everyday Life*. New York: HarperCollins, 1997.

Friedman, M., and Friedman, R. *Free to Choose*. New York: Penguin, 1980.

Glink, I.R. *100 Questions You Should Ask About Your Personal Finances*. New York: Times Books, 1999.

Green, E. *Banking: an Illustrated History*. Oxford: Diane Publishing Co., 1999.

Greer, D.F. *Business, Government, and Society*. Engelwood Cliffs, NJ: Prentice Hall, 1993.

Griffin, R.W., and Ebert, R.J. *Business*. Engelwood Cliffs, NJ: Prentice Hall, 1998.

Hawken, P., et al. *Natural Capitalism: Creating the Next Industrial Revolution*. Boston, MA: Little Brown and Co., 1999.

Hegar, K.W., Pride, W.M., Hughes, R.J., and Kapoor, J. *Business*. Boston: Houghton Mifflin College, 1999.

Heilbroner, R. *The Worldly Philosophers*. New York: Penguin Books, 1991.

Heilbroner, R., and Thurow, L.C. *Economics Explained: Everything You Need to Know About How the Economy Works and Where It's Going*. Touchstone Books, 1998.

Hill, S.D. (ed.). *Consumer Sourcebook*. Detroit, MI: The Gale Group, 1999.

Hirsch, C., Summers, L., and Woods, S.D. *Taxation : Paying for Government*. Austin, TX: Steck-Vaughn Company, 1993.

Houthakker, H.S. *The Economics of Financial Markets*. New York: Oxford University Press, 1996.

Kaufman, H. *Interest Rates, the Markets, and the New Financial World*. New York: Times Books, 1986.

Keynes, J.M. *The General Theory of Employment, Interest, and Money*. New York: Harcourt, Brace, 1936.

Killingsworth, M.R. *Labor Supply*. New York: Cambridge University Press, 1983.

Kosters, M.H. (ed.). *The Effects of Minimum Wage on Employment*. Washington, D.C.: AEI Press, 1996.

Krugman, P.R., and Obstfeld, M. *International Economics: Theory and Policy*. Reading, MA: Addison-Wesley Publishing, 2000.

Landsburg, S.E. *The Armchair Economist: Economics and Everyday Life*. New York: Free Press (Simon and Schuster), 1995.

Lipsey, R.G., Ragan, C.T.S., and Courant, P.N. *Economics*. Reading, MA: Addison Wesley, 1997.

Levine, N. (ed.). *The U.S. and the EU: Economic Relations in a World of Transition*. Lanham, MD: University Press of America, 1996.

MacGregor Burns, J. (ed.). *Government by the People*. Engelwood Cliffs, NJ: Prentice Hall, 1997.

Magnusson, L. *Mercantilism*. New York: Routledge, 1995.

Mayer, T., Duesenberry, J.S., and Aliber, R.Z. *Money, Banking and the Economy*. New York: W.W. Norton and Company, 1996.

Mescon, M.H., Courtland, L.B., and Thill, J.V. *Business Today*. Engelwood Cliffs, NJ: Prentice Hall, 1998.

Morris, K.M, and Siegel, A.M. *The Wall Street Journal Guide to Understanding Personal Finance.* New York: Lightbulb Press Inc, 1997

Naylor, W. Patrick. *10 Steps to Financial Success: a Beginner's Guide to Saving and Investing.* New York: John Wiley & Sons, 1997.

Nelson, B.F., and Stubb, C.G. (ed.) *The European Union : Readings on the Theory and Practice of European Integration.* Boulder, CO: Lynne Rienner Publishers, 1998.

Nicholson, W. *Microeconomic Theory: Basic Principles and Extensions.* Forth Worth, TX: Dryden Press, 1998.

Nordlinger, E.A. *Isolationism Reconfigured: American Foreign Policy for a New Century.* Princeton, NJ: Princeton University Press, 1996.

Painter, D.S. *The Cold War.* New York: Routledge, 1999.

Parkin, M. *Economics.* Reading, MA: Addison-Wesley, 1990.

Parrillo, D.F. *The NASDAQ Handbook.* New York: Probus Publishing, 1992.

Porter, M.E. *On Competition.* Cambridge, MA: Harvard Business School Press, 1998.

Pounds, N.J.G. *An Economic History of Medieval Europe.* Reading, MA: Addison-Wesley, 1994.

Pugh, P., and Garrett, C. *Keynes for Beginners.* Cambridege, U.K.: Icon Books, 1993.

Rima, I.H. *Labor Markets in a Global Economy: An Introduction.* Armonk, NY: M.E. Sharpe, 1996.

Rius *Introducing Marx.* Cambridge, U.K.: Icon Books, 1999.

Rosenberg. J.M. *Dictionary of International Trade.* New York: John Wiley & Sons, 1993.

Rye, D.E. *1,001 Ways to Save, Grow, and Invest Your Money.* Franklin Lakes, NJ: Career Press Inc, 1999.

Rymes, T.K. *The Rise and Fall of Monetarism: The Re-emergence of a Keynesian Monetary Theory and Policy.* Northampton, MA: Edward Elgar Publishing, 1999.

Sachs, J.A., and Larrain, F.B. *Macroeconomics in the Global Economy.* Englewood Cliffs, NJ: Prentice Hall, 1993.

Shapiro, C., and Varian, H.R. *Information Rules: A Strategic Guide to the Network Economy.* Cambridge, MA: Harvard Business School, 1998.

Smith, A. *An Inquiry into the Nature and Causes of the Wealth of Nations,* Edwin Cannan (ed.). Chicago: University of Chicago Press, 1976.

Spulber, N. *The American Economy: the Struggle for Supremacy in the 21st Century.* New York: Cambridge University Press, 1995.

Stubbs, R., and Underhill, G. *Political Economy and the Changing Global Order.* New York: St. Martins Press, 1994.

Teece, D.J. *Economic Performance and the Theory of the Firm.* Northampton, MA: Edward Elgar Publishing, 1998.

Thurow, L.C. *The Future of Capitalism: How Today's Economic Forces Shape Tomorrow's World.* New York: Penguin, USA, 1997.

Tracy, J.A. *Accounting for Dummies.* Foster City, CA: IDG Books Worldwide, 1997.

Tufte, E. R. *Political Control of the Economy.* Princeton, NJ: Princeton University Press, 1978.

Varian, H.R. *Microeconomic Analysis.* New York: W.W. Norton and Company, 1992.

Veblen, T. *The Theory of the Leisure Class (Great Minds Series).* Amherst, NY: Prometheus Books, 1998.

Wallis, J., and Dollery, B. *Market Failure, Government Failure, Leadership and Public Policy.* New York: St. Martin's Press, 1999.

Weaver, C.L. *The Crisis in Social Security: Economic and Political Origins.* Durham, NC: Duke University Press, 1992.

Werner, W., and Smith, S.T. *Wall Street.* New York: Columbia University Press, 1991.

Weygandt, J.J., and Kieso, D.E. (ed.). *Accounting Principles.* New York: John Wiley & Sons Inc, 1996.

Williams, J. (ed.). *Money. A History.* London: British Museum Press, 1997.

Websites

Consumer Product Safety Commission: http://www.cpsc.gov/

Equal Employment Opportunity Commission: http://www.eeoc.gov/

Environmental Protection Agency: http://www.epa.gov/

Federal Reserve System: http://www.federalreserve.gov/

Federal Trade Commission: http://www.ftc.gov/

Food and Drug Administration: http://www.fda.gov/

The Inland Revenue Service: http://www.irs.gov/

Occupational Health and Safety Administration: http://www.osha.gov/

Social Security Administration: http://www.ssa.gov/

The U.S. Chamber of Commerce: http://www.uschamber.com

The U.S. Labor Department: http://www.dol.gov/

The U.S. Treasury Department: http://www.treas.gov/

Picture Credits

Index

Page numbers in **bold** refer to main articles; those in *italics* refer to pictures or their captions.

Fluvanna County High School
1918 Thomas Jefferson Parkway
Palmyra, VA 22963